MW00978948

FAVOURITE CHICKEN
STEP-BY-STEP
RECIPES

Your Promise of Success

Welcome to the world of Confident Cooking,
created for you in the Test Kitchen, where
recipes are double-tested by our team
of home economists to achieve a high
standard of success – and delicious
results every time.

MURDOCH BOOKS®
Sydney • London • Vancouver

CONTE

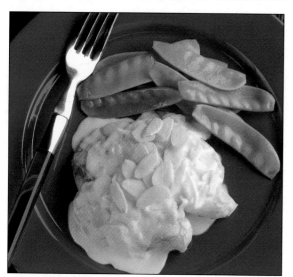

Almond Chicken with Brandy Sauce, page 72.

Crispy Tomato and Onion Chicken, page 30.

Roast Chicken with Bacon and Sage Stuffing, page 31.

Garlic Chicken Kebabs with Tomato and Mushroom Salad, page 40.

N T S

Chicken Burgers with Grainy Mustard Cream, page 35.

Camembert Chicken with Cranberry Sauce, page 66.

The Publisher thanks the following for their assistance in the photography for this book: Barbara's Storehouse; Corso de' Fiori; Country Floors; Home and Garden on the Mall; Inmaterial; I. Redelman & Son; IVV; Krosno; Made on Earth; Mikasa Tableware; Noritake; Pacific East India Company Paraphenalia; Royal Doulton; Villeroy & Boch.

The test kitchen where our recipes are double-tested by our team of home economists to achieve a high standard of success and delicious results every time.

When we test our recipes, we rate them for ease of preparation. The following cookery ratings are on the recipes in this book, making them easy to use and understand.

A single Cooking with Confidence symbol indicates a recipe that is simple and generally quick to make – perfect for beginners.

Two symbols indicate the need for just a little more care and a little more time.

Three symbols indicate special dishes that need more investment in time, care and patience – but the results are worth it.

Front cover: (clockwise from left) Roast Chicken with Breadcrumb Stuffing (p. 24), Chicken and Ham Pie (p. 18) and Mediterranean Chicken Parcels (p. 94).
Inside front cover: Tandoori Chicken on Skewers (top) and Chilli Chicken with Salsa (p. 38).

Baked Chicken Rolls, page 89.

Chicken and Pepperoni Pasta, page 108.

Chicken Basics

Chicken is a versatile food — it lends itself to many different recipes
and styles of cuisine. This guide to purchasing, storing, cooking and presentation
will help you prepare successful and delicious chicken dishes.

Here is advice on how to get the best out of chicken: what to look for when buying and how to store and prepare your purchase prior to cooking. There's also information on how to make stock and gravy, the art of carving, and wines to accompany your meal.

Purchasing

There is a wide variety of chickens and chicken cuts available.

Young tender birds are good for grilling, barbecuing, frying and roasting. Chickens over 1.8 kg are usually only suitable for poaching, braising or boiling because of their tough flesh (although they have excellent flavour) and are labelled as boiling fowls. Unless you specifically want a very large bird, buy two smaller chickens rather than one large.

Whole baby chickens (or poussins) weigh about 500 g and serve one person. Chickens under 1.5 kg serve two to four people. Whole roasting chickens weighing over 1.5 kg should serve at least four people.

Chickens are sold cleaned, with

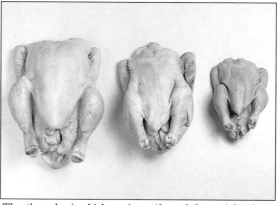

The three basic chicken sizes: (from left to right) large boiling fowl; roasting chicken; baby chicken or poussin.

their innards removed. The neck is usually tucked inside. Sometimes the giblets are in the cavity, contained in a plastic bag, so be sure to remove them before cooking or freezing.

Whole birds are marketed by weight, and the weight becomes the number of the chicken. For example, a No. 10 chicken weighs 1 kg; a No. 16 chicken weighs 1.6 kg, etc.

When buying chicken by weight, check whether the giblets are with the bird. Giblets weigh approximately 175 g and will affect the number of portions you get after cooking.

Fresh chicken

Fresh chicken has better flavour and texture than frozen. Look for skin that is light pink and moist, rather than wet, with no dry spots. It should be unbroken and free from blemishes and bruises. The breast should be plump and well-rounded; on a young bird the point of the breastbone will be flexible.

At specialty poultry shops you can buy free-range, grain-fed, and corn-fed chickens, which have yellow skin and flesh.

Chicken can also be purchased cooked. Hot take-away barbecue, roast or char-grilled chicken has become a mainstay of busy people as the basis for quick and satisfying meals (see page 100). Cooked, smoked chicken is available whole, chilled, from delicatessens and supermarkets.

Chicken cuts include: double or single breasts on the bone, with skin or without; breast fillets; tenderloin (the part just behind the breast); maryland (the whole thigh and leg); thigh cutlets; thigh fillets, wings and

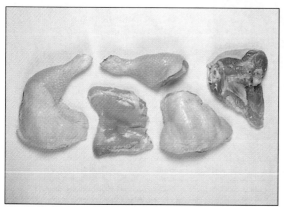

Chicken leg cuts, clockwise from left, maryland, drumstick, thigh (underside view), thigh, thigh fillet.

Chicken breast and wing cuts, clockwise from left, whole breast with bone, single breast fillet, wing, tenderloin.

drumsticks (bottom part of the leg). Buy the appropriate cut of chicken for the cooking process you will be using. Chicken is versatile, and it is not always necessary to buy the most expensive fillets to produce an excellent result. Here is a guide to the cuts used in this book.

For roasting – whole roasting chickens, baby chickens, whole breasts, wings, maryland, drumsticks, thighs.

For grilling – chicken halves and quarters, wings, drumsticks, maryland, thigh cutlets.

For barbecuing – chicken halves, whole breasts, wings, drumsticks, maryland, thigh cutlets, tenderloins.

For stir-frying – breast fillets, thigh fillets, tenderloin, livers.

For pan-frying – maryland, breast fillets, tenderloin, livers.

For deep-frying – drumsticks, wings, thighs, chicken pieces.

For casserole/braising – whole chickens, chicken pieces, thighs, thigh cutlets, drumsticks, wings.

For poaching – whole chicken, whole breasts, breast fillets, thighs, drumsticks.

For stock – bones, necks, giblets, boiling fowls.

Storing fresh chicken: Chicken must be transported home as quickly as possible. Do not leave it sitting in the sun in the car or car boot. The internal temperature of a car left closed in full sun spells disaster to all chicken products. The longer that food spends at temperatures between 5°C and 60°C, the greater the likelihood of rapid growth of harmful bacteria that may result in food poisoning.

Keep chicken away from any strong-smelling items such as cleaning agents and petrol that you may have stored in your vehicle; chicken will absorb the smells.

Make it your policy to purchase chicken or meat as the last item on your round of shopping. In hot weather, use an insulated chiller bag to keep it cold.

It is particularly important to store poultry carefully to avoid contamination by salmonella bacteria, which can cause food poisoning. Always wash hands, chopping boards, knives and cooking implements in very hot soapy water after handling raw chicken. Always keep cooked and raw chicken separate.

Before storing uncooked whole chicken, discard the tight plastic wrappings and pour off any juices. Remove neck and giblets from whole birds (sometimes these are in a plastic bag inside the cavity). Giblets should be cooked immediately or stored separately. Use the neck and giblets for stock; chop the liver to flavour a sauce, gravy or stuffing.

Loosely wrap the chicken in plastic wrap or place in a plastic bag, place package on a plate and refrigerate. Never place uncooked chicken where the juices could drip on or otherwise come in contact with other foodstuffs. A fresh, cleaned and wrapped chicken can be stored in the refrigerator for up to two days.

To store fresh chicken pieces or cuts, remove them from trays or other packaging, pour off any juices and loosely wrap in plastic wrap or place in a plastic bag. Refrigerate for up to two days.

Storing cooked chicken: Chicken should stand no more than an hour at room temperature after cooking. If keeping longer than this, store it loosely wrapped in the refrigerator and use within three days. The chicken does not have to be cold when it goes into the refrigerator. If the chicken has a sauce or stuffing, it should be eaten within 24 hours. Stuffing and gravy should be stored separately.

Frozen chicken

Make sure that any frozen chicken you buy from the supermarket freezer section is solid and completely enclosed in its packaging. Do not purchase any that appear semi-soft and that are sitting in their own drip, as this indicates they have been in the display cabinet for longer than is ideal.

Uncooked, home-frozen chicken (without giblets) will keep for up to nine months in good condition. Remove the giblets before freezing as they will begin to deteriorate after eight weeks.

If a package has partly defrosted it must never be refrozen; defrost fully in the refrigerator and cook promptly. Stuffed birds should never be frozen, as the filling will not freeze enough to prevent the development of harmful bacteria.

Freezing fresh chicken: Have the freezer temperature at minus 15°C or lower. Use heavy gauge polythene bags and good quality plastic wrap to package fresh chicken.

Label each package with the details of the contents, the date it was packaged and stored and either the number of people it will feed or the unfrozen weight. Use a waterproof pen or wax crayon.

It is important to expel as much air as possible from the packaging; oxygen left behind will speed up the process of oxidisation of any fat, resulting in an unpleasant taste after prolonged storing. If you do a lot of freezing, it may be worthwhile investing in a vacuum freezer pump to efficiently expel air.

Secure freezer bags by twisting the tips and closing them with masking tape; this is preferable to metal twist ties. Or, clip a metal band in place with a clipping device.

To freeze uncooked chicken, wrap in heavy-duty plastic bags.

To freeze cooked dishes, place into plastic or aluminium containers.

Trim any pockets of fat from the chicken cavity before cooking.

Wrap the bird in heavy-gauge freezer bags or good quality plastic wrap, then in aluminium foil, expelling air. Label and freeze. Remove the giblets and neck and pack separately to be used for stock.

Commercially frozen whole chickens without giblets can be kept for nine months, or according to instructions on the package. If the chicken is still frozen hard, place it in the freezer in its original wrappings as soon as possible after purchase. If it has started to thaw, place it in the refrigerator to completely thaw out, cook it promptly, cool quickly, wrap and refreeze it. Never re-freeze thawed, uncooked poultry.

Whole birds can be trussed before freezing to be ready for cooking when thawed. To provide convenient serving portions and to save space, cut the chicken into four, eight or 10 pieces before freezing. Wrap each joint individually in plastic wrap, expelling air, and then combine in a larger package in a sturdy plastic bag. Seal, tape the end of the bag to the package, label and freeze.

Chicken cuts such as legs or wings can be frozen either as individual portions or in amounts to serve several people. Wrap portions individually in plastic wrap, expelling air, then place them in a larger plastic bag. Seal and tape the end of the bag to the package. Label and freeze.

Boneless cuts can be cut into strips or cubes before freezing. Weigh out meal-size portions and place in heavy duty plastic bags. Fill right to the corners with meat. Flatten the package (so it will defrost quickly) and expel air. Seal, label and freeze.

The same procedure applies to chicken mince.

Stuffing and Trussing

Make up the stuffing according to the recipe. Spoon the stuffing mixture into the tail cavity, filling loosely to allow for expansion during cooking. Secure the skin across the cavity with a skewer, or truss the bird as described below. Stuffing can also be pushed under the skin of the breast and into the neck cavity.

Trussing, or securing a whole bird with string, keeps in the stuffing and holds the bird compactly, so that legs or wing tips do not overcook, and so that the cooked bird sits neatly for carving.

After stuffing the bird, pull the skin down over the opening. Turn the bird onto its breast and tie a long length of string right around the wings, securing them neatly. Turn the bird over, taking the string over the legs and crossing it under the chicken. Tuck the tail (the parson's nose) into the cavity and tie the legs together. After the chicken has been cooked and left to rest for 10 minutes, remove the trussing, then carve.

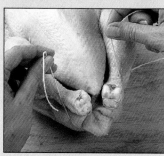

Freezing cooked chicken: Cooked whole chicken or chicken pieces can be frozen with or without bones, for up to two weeks. After this time it will tend to dry out.

Moist chicken dishes such as casseroles, stews, curries and soups are all suitable for freezing. Quickly reduce the temperature of the cooked item by placing it in the refrigerator or by plunging the base of the dish into cold water, then cool completely in the refrigerator. Line cake tins or other suitable containers with a heavy duty plastic bag. Spoon individual portions or meal-size serves

To remove skin from drumsticks, carefully loosen skin at the joint end.

Pull the skin back and away from the flesh of the drumstick.

into the bag and expel air. Seal, label and freeze. Place bag in its tin into the freezer. When frozen, remove from tin, reseal to remove as much air as possible and return, labelled, to the freezer.

Or, simply spoon the meat directly into plastic or aluminium containers and seal, label and freeze. As a general rule, freeze cooked chicken for a maximum of two months.

Defrosting: Frozen chicken must be completely thawed in the refrigerator before cooking; allow two to three hours per 500 g. A frozen bird should be cooked within 12 hours of thawing. Do not thaw chicken at room temperature. Never keep perishable food at room temperature for longer than two hours, particularly on hot days. This includes time to prepare, serve and eat.

Microwave defrosting is not recommended for whole frozen chickens because of uneven thawing. However, smaller packages of cuts or pre-cooked meals can be successfully thawed in the microwave using the defrost setting. Always remove chicken from wrapping before defrosting. Stir casseroles occasionally to distribute heat evenly. Separate joints or pieces as they soften.

Preparation

Before cooking a whole chicken remove neck, giblets and pockets of fat from the cavity. Discard fat, use neck and giblets for stock. Remove any excess fat and sinew from chicken pieces.

Raw poultry should be wiped over with a damp cloth, rather than washed, before cooking. Wipe commercially frozen birds with paper towels to absorb excess moisture.

Use a cook's knife for jointing

Jointing

Jointing a whole chicken is an easy process, once you know how. Large birds can be cut into four, six, eight or 10 pieces. Legs should be cut into smaller pieces than the breast, as dark meat cooks more slowly than light. Use a sharp, heavy knife or poultry shears.

To cut a bird into six pieces, remove the leg by cutting around the end of the thigh joint. Twist the leg sharply outwards to break the joint, and then cut

through the joint. Turn the bird around and repeat on the other side. Remove the wings by bending them outwards and snipping around the joint. Cut up one side of the body and open it out flat. Cut the body into two pieces. Cut down the centre of the breast.

To make eight portions, separate the thigh from drumstick.

To make 10 portions, cut the breast pieces in half.

To marinate, pour liquid over the chicken in a non-metallic dish.

uncooked chickens. Poultry shears are excellent for dividing whole chickens into serving portions. They are especially good for splitting the breastbone, cutting backbone and rib bones and cutting the breast and legs in half.

Stuffing a whole chicken before roasting adds flavour and plumps up the bird. Do not stuff a bird more than three hours before cooking. If using warm stuffing, cook the bird immediately. Stuffed, or stuffed and trussed birds take a little longer to cook than unstuffed.

Some people prefer chicken without the skin. Removing the skin eliminates any fat from the chicken, as the fat lies in a layer just underneath the skin. Usually the skin is removed after cooking, but drumsticks can be skinned and then cooked. To remove the skin from drumsticks, use a small sharp knife. Begin by carefully loosening the skin from the flesh at the large joint end. Then pull the skin down and away from the flesh. Some chicken shops sell drumsticks with the skin already removed.

Boning a whole chicken is a technique used for special-occasion dishes. With the bones removed, the chicken makes a meaty casing for a luxurious stuffing and the cooked bird is easy to carve or slice. Chicken presented in this way is often served cold. Chicken wings can also be boned and stuffed, making an easy-to-eat appetiser or finger food for parties.

Marinating chicken gives it extra flavour and moisture. Marinades usually contain at least one acid ingredient, such as wine, vinegar, lemon juice or even yoghurt, to tenderise, plus other ingredients to flavour and colour the chicken.

Boning whole chicken

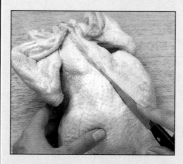 

To bone chicken: Using a small, sharp knife, cut through the skin on the centre back. Separate the flesh from the bone down one side to the breast, being careful not to pierce skin. Follow along the bones closely with the

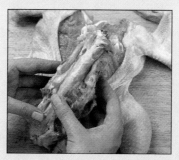 

knife, gradually easing meat from thigh, drumstick and wing. Cut through thigh bone and cut off wing tip. Repeat on the other side, then lift the rib cage away, leaving the flesh in one piece. Scrape all the meat from the drum-

 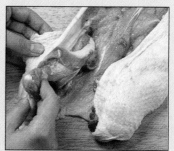

stick and wings; discard bones. Turn the wing and drumstick flesh inside the chicken and lay chicken out flat, skin-side down. The chicken is now ready to be stuffed and rolled according to the recipe.

Marinating is ideal to use in conjunction with quick-cooking methods. Frozen chicken should be thawed before marinating.

Place chicken in a shallow ceramic or glass (not metal) container and pour in the marinade. Stir well to make sure chicken is well coated. Cover with plastic wrap and refrigerate, usually for at least two to eight hours, or preferably overnight, turning occasionally. When ready to cook, drain chicken and reserve liquid (or discard, according to the particular recipe) for basting during cooking and for making a sauce to serve with the finished dish. Honey or sugar should be used sparingly in marinades as sweet mixtures easily scorch during cooking.

Boning Wings

Boned chicken wings can be stuffed with a variety of ingredients and are easier to eat than unboned wings. Smaller wings make excellent barbecued or pan-fried entrees. Use larger wings for main course dishes.

Using a small sharp knife and starting at the drumstick end, slip knife down sides of bone towards the joint, without piercing the skin. Snap the bone free and proceed with the next joint in the same way, taking care not to pierce the elbow. Remove the bones and reshape the wing ready for stuffing.

Cooking Techniques

Chicken must always be eaten thoroughly cooked. To test when roast, grilled or barbecued poultry is cooked, insert a skewer into the thickest part of the bird (the thigh). If the juices run clear, the chicken is done. You can also test for doneness by twisting or jiggling the leg. If it moves easily in its socket the chicken is cooked. Pan-fried, grilled or barbecued chicken is cooked when meat is tender enough to fall easily off the bone when tested with a fork.

There are two cooking methods, using either dry heat or moist heat.

Dry heat cookery comprises oven roasting, barbecuing and grilling, stir-frying and pan-frying. With these methods, timing is important to prevent a tough, dry result.

Moist heat cookery comprises braising, casseroling, pot roasting, poaching and steaming. The less tender cuts are ideal here because they benefit from the long, slow cooking.

Roasting: Stuff and truss the chicken if desired. Preheat the oven and have the bird at room temperature. Use a shallow ovenproof pan that fits the bird without squeezing it in. Place chicken on a rack in the pan, and put a little wine or water in the bottom of the pan, if liked, to prevent the bird drying out. Brush all over with melted butter or oil. If the breast is browning too quickly, cover with a piece of aluminium foil. Cook according to directions in the recipe, basting occasionally. After roasting, let the bird rest for 10 minutes, covered loosely with foil, before carving.

Barbecuing: Give the barbecue plenty of time to heat up, so that the chicken is cooking over glowing coals rather than flames. Cooking times will depend on the thickness of the chicken pieces. There is a tendency for the outside of the chicken to cook too fast when barbecued. If this happens, move the pieces further away from the heat, or brown the outside and then continue cooking wrapped in foil. Serve wrapped in foil to preserve the juices. Brush unwrapped pieces with marinade, butter or oil during cooking to prevent drying out.

To barbecue, place chicken on a preheated grill. Brush with marinade.

Grilling: Preheat the grill and place chicken pieces on a cold, oiled grill-pan. Arrange pieces skin-side down and cook about 10 cm from heat source for 15 to 20 minutes, then turn and cook second side until the juices run clear when tested with a skewer. Brush with marinade during cooking to prevent chicken drying out. If not using a marinade, chicken can be brushed with butter, herb butter or oil during cooking.

Stir-frying: This is the traditional Asian way of cooking meat. This rapid method uses neatly cut strips of chicken, trimmed of fat and sinew. The strips must be evenly cut so that they cook at the same rate. Heat a little oil in a wok or large heavy-based

To roast, place on a rack in an oven tray. Brush with melted butter or oil.

Insert a skewer into thigh; if juice runs clear the chicken is cooked.

To stir-fry, toss even-sized chicken pieces over high heat in wok or pan.

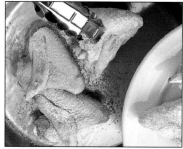

To pan-fry, cook in a single layer without crowding the pan.

To deep-fry, cook pieces in hot oil. When ready, remove and drain.

frying pan and tilt the pan so that the bottom and sides are evenly coated. Stir-fry by tossing chicken quickly in small batches over high heat until cooked.

Pan-frying: This method is best for small, tender chickens. Heat oil or butter in a heavy-based pan on high heat, add chicken pieces and cook for 2–3 minutes on each side to brown and seal in juices, turning with tongs. Reduce heat, cover pan if necessary and cook as directed. Do not crowd the pan. Use a wide, heavy-based pan or two smaller pans so the chicken will fit in a single layer rather than trying to fit too much into one pan. If the chicken is cooked without a coating, pat pieces dry with paper towels before cooking. Put pieces with bone in flesh-side first, as the side that cooks first looks the best when serving.

Deep-frying: Preheat a deep pan half filled with oil. Test oil by dropping a square of dry bread into it. If the bread browns within 15 seconds and the oil bubbles and sizzles, it is hot enough for cooking. Chicken pieces should be of equal size so that they will cook at the same time. Dip chicken pieces firstly in water, drain, then in flour and/or breadcrumbs, then lower into the hot oil. When cooked, lift out with tongs and drain on paper towels.

Casseroling and braising: This long, slow cooking process brings out the best in chicken, and will transform even a 'tough old bird' into a meltingly delicious dish. The chicken should be gently simmered, never boiled, in the cooking liquid – boiling will make the chicken flesh tough. Brown whole birds or pieces in butter or oil, then transfer to an oven- or flame-proof dish, with vegetables and cooking liquids such as stock and wine. If cooked on top of the stove the dish is covered, brought quickly to the boil, then heat

Carving

Let the cooked bird stand for 10 minutes in a warm place, covered loosely with foil. (This rests the meat and makes it easier to carve.) Place on a carving board or secure surface. Using a two-pronged fork to hold the bird and a sharp carving knife, cut around the leg, taking in a reasonable amount of flesh from the sides, firstly cutting through the skin and then using the tip of the knife to separate the bone at the joint. Cut above the wing joint, through the breastbone. Separate legs by cutting into thigh and drumstick. Carve breast meat in slices parallel to the rib cage. Place pieces on a warmed serving platter with vegetables or directly onto serving plates. Give each person some white and dark meat.

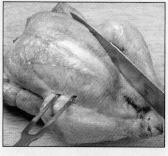

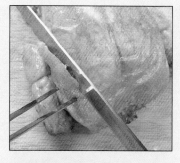

To casserole or braise, chicken is first browned quickly to seal in juices.

To poach, simmer chicken gently in wine or water until tender.

is reduced to a simmer – small bubbles should gently break the surface. For oven cooking, cover the pot and cook at a temperature low enough to prevent the liquid boiling.

Poaching: In this method, the chicken is gently simmered in water, stock or wine, sometimes with vegetables and herbs added for flavour. The cooking liquid must never boil. This is a suitable method for cooking large chickens. If using a smaller bird, reduce the cooking time. After cooking, the liquid is strained and used to make a sauce to accompany the chicken or reserved for stock. Because of the low fat content, especially if skin is removed, poached chicken is ideal for dieters.

Wines to serve with chicken

White wines are the perfect complement for chicken, with different styles suiting different dishes. White wines should be served well chilled. In hot weather, place the bottle in an ice bucket or wine cooler.

Light, fresh fruity wines, such as moselle and sauvignon blanc are perfect with cold chicken.

Stronger-flavoured white wines with more body, and matured wines, such as aged oaky Australian chardonnays, gewurtztraminer, frascati from Italy, semillon and rieslings, are well matched with savoury, rich and flavoursome chicken dishes.

Some lighter reds can be drunk with chicken. A chilled rosé can accompany salads and cold dishes, while beaujolais-style wines go well with chicken burgers or pan-fried or barbecued chicken.

Sparkling wines, such as dry champagne, are excellent partners for creamy chicken dishes.

Chicken Stock

Many recipes in this book call for chicken stock. This pantry basic is easy to prepare at home and imparts the best flavour to the dishes it is used in.

Chicken stock can be refrigerated or frozen in convenient amounts for up to eight weeks. Fill ice-cube trays with stock and freeze so that you can use a small amount for a sauce or to add to baby's mixed vegetables. For recipes that call for large amounts of stock, such as soups or stews, measure the stock by the cup into plastic containers, label them and freeze.

Chicken bones for making stock can be purchased from butchers and specialty chicken stores. The neck and giblets removed from a whole roasting chicken can also be added for extra flavour.

If light chicken stock is specified in a recipe, dilute the basic stock with one-third water or until it reaches the desired strength.

Chicken stock can be purchased frozen from some specialty chicken shops or packaged in tetra-packs from supermarkets. Tinned consommé can be substituted. Chicken stock cubes and powder are also available.

Chicken Stock
Makes 4 cups

500 g chicken bones
1 large onion, chopped
1 carrot, chopped
1 stick celery (leaves included), chopped
2 bay leaves
6 peppercorns
4–5 cups water

➤ PREHEAT OVEN to moderate 180°C.
1 Place the chicken bones and onions in a baking dish. Bake for 50 minutes or until well browned. Transfer the bones and onions to large pan or stockpot.
2 Wrap bay leaves and peppercorns in a piece of muslin to make a bouquet garni. Add remaining ingredients with bouquet garni to pan. Bring to boil, reduce heat and simmer, uncovered, for 40 minutes, adding a little more water if necessary. Strain stock. Discard bones and vegetables. Cool quickly and refrigerate or freeze. After refrigeration, skim any hard fat that may have risen to the surface. Use stock as indicated in recipe.

Traditional chicken gravy

A rich, delicious gravy to serve with roast chicken is easily achieved. This recipe makes enough gravy to serve 4–6 people. A little white wine, marsala, or chopped fresh herbs or mushrooms can be added to the recipe. Store leftover gravy separately from chicken, in the refrigerator.

To make gravy: Sprinkle 2 tablespoons plain flour evenly over an oven tray. Place under a hot grill until flour is golden. Add the flour to the pan juices from the roasting chicken, stir over low heat for 2 minutes. Add 3/4 cup of chicken stock gradually to pan, stirring until the mixture is smooth. Stir constantly over medium heat for 5 minutes or until gravy boils and thickens; boil a further 1 minute and remove from heat. Pour into a warmed sauce boat and serve hot with chicken.

FAMILY FAVOURITES

CHICKEN AND SPINACH LASAGNE

Preparation time: 30 minutes
Total cooking time: 1 hour 10 minutes
Serves 8

1 bunch English spinach
1 tablespoon oil
1 kg chicken mince
1 clove garlic, crushed
3 bacon rashers, chopped
425 g can tomatoes
2¼ cups tomato paste
½ cup tomato sauce
½ cup chicken stock
salt and freshly ground black
    pepper, to taste
12 instant lasagne sheets
1 cup grated cheddar cheese

Cheese Sauce
60 g butter
⅓ cup plain flour
2½ cups milk
1 cup grated cheddar cheese

➤ PREHEAT OVEN to moderate 180°C. Remove stalks from spinach leaves; discard. Plunge leaves in a medium pan of boiling water 2 minutes or until tender. Remove, plunge into bowl of iced water; drain.
1 Heat oil in a heavy-based frying pan; add mince, garlic and bacon.

Cook over medium heat 5 minutes or until well browned. Stir in undrained, crushed tomatoes, tomato paste, sauce and stock; bring to boil. Reduce heat and simmer, partially covered, 10 minutes, or until sauce is slightly thickened. Season to taste.
2 To make Cheese Sauce: Heat butter in medium pan; add flour. Stir over low heat 1 minute or until mixture is lightly golden. Add milk gradually to pan, stirring until smooth. Stir constantly over medium heat 4 minutes or until sauce boils and thickens. Remove from heat; stir in cheese.
3 To assemble lasagne: Brush a deep, rectangular ovenproof dish (12-cup capacity) with melted butter or oil. Spread one-quarter of the chicken mixture over base of dish. Top with four sheets of lasagne. Spread with one-third of the cheese sauce, then half the chicken mixture. Top with all the spinach, a layer of lasagne, half the remaining sauce and all of the remaining chicken mixture. Arrange remaining lasagne sheets over chicken mixture. Spread evenly with remaining cheese sauce and sprinkle with grated cheese. Bake for 50 minutes or until cooked through and golden brown.

COOK'S FILE

Storage time: This dish can be made a day ahead and refrigerated. Reheat in oven just before serving.

2

3

CHICKEN AND VEGETABLE HOT POT

Preparation time: 20 minutes
Total cooking time: 35 minutes
Serves 4

8 (1.5 kg) chicken thigh cutlets
1/2 cup plain flour
cracked black pepper, to taste
2 tablespoons oil
1 medium onion, sliced
1 clove garlic, crushed
4 bacon rashers, chopped
2 medium potatoes, peeled and
    cut into 1.5 cm cubes
1 large carrot, chopped
1 celery stick, cut into wide
    slices

2 medium zucchini, sliced
300 g cauliflower, cut into
    small florets
425 g can tomatoes
2 tablespoons tomato paste
2/3 cup red wine
2/3 cup chicken stock (see
    page 11)
salt and freshly ground black
    pepper, to taste

➤ TRIM CHICKEN of excess fat and
sinew. Combine flour and pepper on
a sheet of greaseproof paper.
1 Toss chicken lightly in seasoned
flour; shake off excess. Heat oil in a
large heavy-based pan. Cook chicken
over medium heat, turning occasionally, until browned and cooked through.
Drain on paper towels; keep warm.

2 Add onion, garlic and bacon to
pan. Cook, stirring, until onion is soft.
Add potatoes, carrot and celery and
cook, stirring, 2 minutes. Add vegetables, undrained crushed tomatoes,
tomato paste, wine and stock. Season
to taste. Bring to boil; reduce heat.
Simmer, covered, 10 minutes, stirring
occasionally, or until the sauce is
slightly thickened and vegetables are
tender. Do not overcook vegetables.
3 Add chicken to sauce mixture,
gently stir until heated through.

COOK'S FILE

Storage time: Cook this dish just
before serving. The chicken can be
prepared a day ahead and stored,
covered, in refrigerator. Reheat just
before adding to vegetable mixture.

LEMON CHICKEN

Preparation time: 15 minutes
Total cooking time: 1 hour 10 minutes
Serves 4

1.6 kg chicken
1 tablespoon soy sauce
1 tablespoon dry sherry
1 tablespoon lemon juice
2 teaspoons soft brown sugar

Lemon Sauce
2 spring onions
1/2 cup lemon juice
1/2 cup caster sugar
2 teaspoons dry sherry
1 teaspoon soy sauce
1 tablespoon cornflour
1/2 cup water
salt and white pepper, to taste

➤ PREHEAT OVEN to moderate 180°C. Remove the giblets and any large deposits of fat from the chicken. Wipe chicken and pat dry with paper towels.

1 Tie wings and drumsticks securely in place. Place chicken on a rack in baking dish. Brush with combined soy sauce, sherry, juice and sugar.

2 Bake chicken 1 hour or until juices run clear when the flesh is pierced with a skewer. Baste occasionally with remaining soy mixture. Remove from oven and leave, covered with foil, in a warm place 10 minutes. Remove string before serving. Serve hot with Lemon Sauce and steamed rice or noodles.

3 Cut spring onions into long thin strips; place in iced water until curly.

4 To make Lemon Sauce: Combine juice, sugar, sherry and soy sauce in small pan. Blend cornflour with water in small bowl or jug until smooth. Add to pan. Stir over medium heat 4 minutes or until sauce boils and thickens slightly. Season to taste; stir in spring onions.

COOK'S FILE

Storage time: Cook this dish just before serving.

Variation: This dish can be made using chicken breast fillets. Cut fillets into strips, combine with soy mixture. Drain chicken, stir-fry in wok or frying pan until cooked but not browned. Make sauce as directed, combine with chicken strips and serve.

1

2

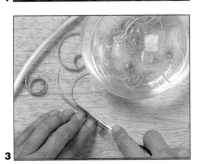
3

4

CHICKEN AND MACARONI BAKE

Preparation time: 20 minutes
Total cooking time: 55 minutes
Serves 6

2 cups macaroni
1/4 cup olive oil
4 (460 g) chicken breast fillets
1 medium onion, chopped
1 medium carrot, chopped
3 rashers bacon, chopped
2 medium zucchini, chopped

440 g can tomato soup
1/3 cup sour cream
salt and freshly ground black
     pepper, to taste
1 1/2 cups grated cheddar cheese

➤ TRIM CHICKEN of excess fat and sinew. Preheat oven to moderate 180°C. Cook macaroni in large pan of rapidly boiling water with a little oil added until just tender; drain.
1 Slice chicken breasts into long strips and then cut into cubes.
2 Heat oil in heavy-based pan. Cook chicken quickly over high heat until browned but not cooked through; drain on paper towels. Add onion, carrot and bacon to pan. Stir over medium heat 10 minutes; add zucchini and soup. Bring to boil; simmer, uncovered, 5 minutes. Remove from heat.
3 Combine pasta, chicken, tomato mixture and cream. Season to taste. Spread into a shallow ovenproof dish, top with cheese. Bake for 20 minutes or until golden and cooked through.

COOK'S FILE

Storage time: This dish can be made one day ahead and refrigerated.

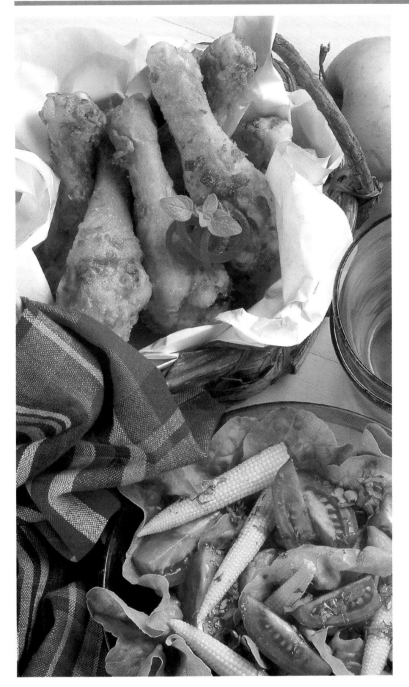

COUNTRY-FRIED CHICKEN

Preparation time: 10 minutes
Total cooking time: 16 minutes
Serves 6

**12 (1.3 kg) chicken drumsticks
1/4 cup finely crushed
    cornflakes
1¼ cups plain flour
2 tablespoons chicken stock
    powder
1 teaspoon celery salt
1 teaspoon onion salt
1/2 teaspoon garlic powder
1/2 teaspoon ground white
    pepper
oil for deep frying**

➤ PLACE CHICKEN in large pan of boiling water; reduce heat and simmer, uncovered, 8 minutes or until chicken is almost cooked through. Lift out with tongs ; drain.

1 Combine cornflakes and sifted flour, stock powder, celery salt and onion salt in a medium bowl. Place drumsticks in large bowl and cover with cold water.

2 Dip wet drumsticks one at a time into the seasoned flour mixture; shake off excess.

3 Heat oil in deep heavy-based pan. Gently lower chicken into moderately hot oil. Cook over medium-high heat for 8 minutes or until golden and cooked through. Carefully remove chicken from oil with tongs or slotted spoon. Drain on paper towels and keep warm. Repeat with remaining chicken pieces. Serve hot.

C O O K ' S   F I L E

Storage time: Cook this dish just before serving.
Hint: Pre-cooking the chicken before frying ensures that it will be cooked through without the skin burning.

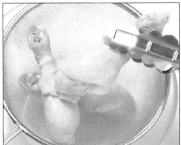

1

2

3

CHICKEN AND HAM PIE

Preparation time: 30 minutes
Total cooking time: 1 hour
Serves 6

375 g packet frozen shortcrust
   pastry
6 (660 g) chicken thigh fillets
2 tablespoons oil
60 g butter
1 medium onion, chopped
1/3 cup plain flour
1 1/2 cups milk
1 tablespoon seeded mustard
1 cup grated cheddar cheese
150 g lean leg ham, chopped
1/2 large red capsicum,
   finely chopped
3 spring onions, chopped
salt and freshly ground black
   pepper, to taste
2 hard-boiled eggs, quartered
375 g packet frozen puff pastry
1 egg, beaten

➤ PREHEAT OVEN to moderately
hot 210°C/190°C gas. Brush a deep,
22 cm round fluted flan tin with melted butter or oil.

1 Roll shortcrust pastry out on a
lightly floured surface large enough to
cover base and sides of prepared tin.

2 Ease pastry into the tin. Cut a
sheet of greaseproof paper large
enough to cover pastry-lined tin.
Spread a layer of dried beans or rice
evenly over paper. Bake for 7 minutes. Remove from oven; discard
paper and beans. Return pastry to
oven for a further 8 minutes or until
lightly golden; cool.

3 Trim chicken of excess fat and
sinew. Cut into 2 cm pieces. Heat oil
in a heavy-based frying pan. Add
chicken and cook in small batches
over medium heat until lightly
browned and cooked through; drain
on paper towels.

4 Heat butter in medium heavy-
based pan. Add the onion and cook
for 2 minutes or until onion is soft.
Add flour and stir over low heat for
1 minute or until mixture is lightly
golden. Add milk gradually to pan,
stirring until mixture is smooth. Stir
constantly over medium heat until
sauce boils and thickens; remove
from heat. Stir in mustard and
cheese; cool slightly. Add the ham,
capsicum, spring onions and chicken
to the sauce mixture, season to taste;
stir gently until well combined.

5 Spoon half the mixture into the
prepared pastry case. Top with quartered eggs, then remaining chicken
mixture. Shape mixture with a large
spoon, forming a rounded top.

6 Roll puff pastry out on a lightly
floured surface, large enough to
cover top of pie. Brush edge of
cooked pastry shell with beaten egg.
Top with puff pastry and press
down edge to seal; trim. Brush top
with egg. Decorate pie with trim-
mings from pastry, if liked. Reduce
oven temperature to moderate 180°C.
Bake 45 minutes or until pastry is
golden brown. Serve hot.

COOK'S FILE

Storage time: Pie can be assembled
one day ahead up to the final baking.
Store, covered with plastic wrap, in
the refrigerator. Remove from refrigerator, bake 45 minutes as directed,
then serve.

Variations: Cooked, lean bacon can
be substituted for ham in this recipe.
Cooked chicken, such as steamed or
leftover roast, can be used instead of
thigh fillets. Remove any skin, bones
or gristle, cut into 2 cm pieces and
use as directed.

Hint: Accompanied by a dollop of
sour cream, a sprig of a fresh herb
and a warmed bread roll, this pie
becomes a dress-up lunch dish. Serve
with a chilled white wine.

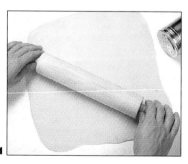
1

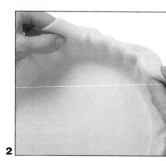
2

3

4

5

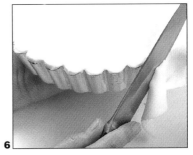
6

CHICKEN AND TOMATO RISOTTO

Preparation time: 15 minutes
Total cooking time: 35 minutes
Serves 4

8 (1 kg) mixed chicken pieces
1/4 cup olive oil
2 large onions, chopped
2 large carrots, cut into
**   1 cm cubes**
1 cup short-grain rice
50 g sachet tomato soup

4 cups chicken stock (see
**   page 11)**
salt and freshly ground black
**   pepper, to taste**
2 tablespoons finely chopped
**   fresh coriander**

➤ TRIM CHICKEN of excess fat and sinew.

1 Heat oil in large heavy-based pan; add chicken pieces. Cook over medium heat 5 minutes or until golden brown, turning once. Remove from pan; drain on paper towels.

2 Add onion and carrot to pan, stir over medium heat 5 minutes or until golden. Add rice and stir over low heat for 5 minutes.

3 Blend the soup mix with the stock and pour into pan. Stir until mixture boils. Return chicken to pan, reduce heat. Simmer, covered, 20 minutes or until the chicken is tender, rice cooked and liquid absorbed, stirring occasionally. Add salt, pepper and coriander just before serving.

COOK'S FILE

Storage time: Cook this dish just before serving.

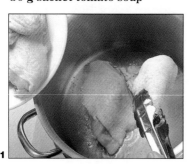
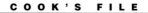

CHICKEN WITH TARRAGON AND MUSHROOMS

Preparation time: 10 minutes
Total cooking time: 50 minutes
Serves 6

6 large (700 g) chicken breast
    fillets, skin removed
1/4 cup olive oil
3 rashers bacon, cut into strips
300 g button mushrooms,
    thinly sliced
1/2 cup dry white wine
2 tablespoons tomato paste
1 teaspoon dried tarragon
1/2 cup cream
3 spring onions, finely chopped
salt and freshly ground black
    pepper, to taste

➤ TRIM CHICKEN of excess fat and sinew.

1 Preheat oven to moderate 180°C. Heat oil in a large heavy-based pan; add chicken. Cook over medium-high heat 2 minutes each side, turning once. Remove from pan; drain.

2 Add bacon to pan. Stir over medium heat 2 minutes; add mushrooms. Cook 5 minutes; add wine, paste and tarragon to pan. Stir until mixture boils. Reduce heat and add cream; simmer 2 minutes. Remove from heat, stir in spring onions. Season to taste.

3 Arrange chicken over base of shallow ovenproof dish. Pour sauce over chicken. Bake, covered, for 30 minutes or until chicken is tender.

COOK'S FILE

Storage time: Cook this dish just before serving.

1

2

3

SAVOURY CHICKEN LOAF

Preparation time: 30 minutes
+ 15 minutes refrigeration
Total cooking time: 1 hour 5 minutes
Serves 4

40 g butter, melted
1¹/2 cups plain flour
1 cup self-raising flour
80 g butter, chopped
²/3 cup water

Filling
1 tablespoon olive oil
3 rashers bacon, chopped
250 g frozen leaf spinach
    portions
500 g chicken mince
1 large tomato, peeled, seeded,
    finely chopped
1 red chilli, finely chopped
1 cup grated cheddar cheese
2 tablespoons self-raising flour
1 egg, lightly beaten
¹/4 cup finely chopped fresh
    continental parsley

salt and freshly ground black
pepper, to taste

➤ PREHEAT OVEN to moderately
hot 210°C/190°C gas. Brush a deep
21 x 14 cm loaf tin with melted butter or oil.
1 Place flours and chopped butter in
food processor bowl. Using the pulse
action, process for 20 seconds or until
mixture is fine and crumbly. Add
water a little at a time; process 15 seconds or until a soft dough forms.
2 Turn dough onto a lightly floured
surface. Knead for 1 minute or until
smooth. Roll three-quarters of the
dough large enough to cover base
and extend over sides of tin. Ease
pastry into tin. Cover with plastic
wrap and refrigerate 15 minutes.
3 **To make Filling:** Heat oil in a
medium heavy-based pan; add bacon.
Stir over medium heat 8 minutes or
until browned. Add frozen spinach.
Cook, covered, 12 minutes or until
spinach defrosts, stirring occasionally.
Cook, uncovered, 5 minutes, stirring
constantly. Remove from heat; cool.
Combine spinach mixture with re-

maining filling ingredients. Season.
4 Spoon filling into prepared tin,
pressing into corners. Roll out remaining dough large enough to cover tin.
Pinch dough edges together. Cut slits
in top of loaf. Brush with remaining
melted butter. Bake 40 minutes or
until well browned and cooked
through. Leave in tin 15 minutes
before turning out. Serve hot or cold.

COOK'S FILE

Storage time: Cook this dish on
day of serving. Store in refrigerator.

MUSHROOM-STUFFED CHICKEN WITH HERB BUTTER

Preparation time: 20 minutes
  + 10 minutes standing
Total cooking time: 1 hour 40 minutes
Serves 6

2 tablespoons olive oil
1 large onion, finely chopped
2 cups (200 g) finely chopped
  mushrooms
1/3 cup chopped sun-dried
  tomatoes
1/3 cup short-grain rice
1 tablespoon tomato paste
1 cup chicken stock (see
  page 11)
1/2 cup peeled and coarsely
  grated apple
1.4 kg chicken

salt and freshly ground black
  pepper, to taste
2 tablespoons melted butter

Herb Butter
100 g butter, softened
2 teaspoons tomato paste
2 teaspoons dried Italian herbs
1/2 teaspoon cracked black
  peppercorns

➤ PREHEAT OVEN to moderate 180°C.
1 Heat oil in medium heavy-based pan; add onion. Stir over medium heat for 5 minutes or until soft. Add mushrooms, cook on high heat 7 minutes or until well browned. Add sun-dried tomatoes, rice, tomato paste and chicken stock; bring to boil. Reduce heat and, simmer, covered, 8 minutes, stirring occasionally. Remove from heat; stir in apple.

2 Remove giblets and any large deposits of fat from chicken. Wipe and pat dry chicken with paper towels. Spoon stuffing into chicken cavity; close cavity with a toothpick or skewer. Tie wings and drumsticks securely in place with string. Rub chicken all over with pepper. Place on roasting rack in a deep baking dish; brush with butter. Roast the chicken for 1 hour 25 minutes or until browned and tender. Remove from oven and leave, loosely covered with foil, in a warm place 10 minutes; remove toothpick and string before serving. Serve hot accompanied by Herb Butter.
3 **To make Herb Butter:** Beat combined ingredients with a wooden spoon until light and creamy.

COOK'S FILE

Storage time: Cook this dish just before serving.

ROAST CHICKEN WITH BREADCRUMB STUFFING

Preparation time: 25 minutes
+ 5 minutes standing
Total cooking time: 1 hour 30 minutes
Serves 6

3 rashers bacon, finely chopped
6 slices wholegrain bread,
    crusts removed
3 spring onions, chopped
2 tablespoons chopped pecan
    nuts
2 teaspoons currants
1/4 cup finely chopped parsley
1/4 cup milk
1 egg, lightly beaten
salt and freshly ground black
    pepper, to taste
1.4 kg chicken
freshly ground black pepper
40 g butter, melted
1 tablespoon oil
1 tablespoon soy sauce
1 1/2 cups water
1 clove garlic crushed
1 tablespoon plain flour

➤ PREHEAT OVEN to moderately
hot 210°C/190°C gas.

1 Cook bacon in a small pan over
high heat 5 minutes or until crisp.
Chop bread into 1 cm squares; place
into large mixing bowl. Add bacon,
spring onions, nuts, currants, parsley
and combined egg and milk to bowl;
season to taste and mix well.

2 Remove the giblets and any large
deposits of fat from the chicken.
Wipe and pat dry chicken with
paper towels. Spoon stuffing into
chicken cavity; close cavity with a
skewer or toothpick. Tie wings and
drumsticks securely in place with
string. Rub chicken all over with salt
and pepper.

3 Place on roasting rack in deep
baking dish. Brush with combined
butter, oil and soy sauce; pour leftover butter mixture, half the water
and garlic into baking dish. Roast
chicken for 1 hour and 15 minutes or
until browned and tender. Baste occasionally with pan juices during cooking. Transfer chicken to a serving dish.
Leave, loosely covered with foil, in a
warm place for 5 minutes before carving. Serve with gravy and vegetables.

4 To make gravy: Transfer baking pan to stovetop. Add flour to pan
juices; blend to a smooth paste. Stir
constantly over low heat 5 minutes or
until mixture browns. Add remaining
water, stir until mixture boils and
thickens. (Add extra water if necessary.) Season to taste; strain into a
serving jug. Serve hot.

COOK'S FILE

Storage time: Cook this dish just
before serving.
Variation: Substitute white wine for
half the water in gravy, if liked.

PINEAPPLE AND CAPSICUM CHICKEN

Preparation time: 10 minutes
Total cooking time: 30 minutes
Serves 4

12 small chicken wings
2 tablespoons cornflour
1/2 teaspoon ground ginger
1 teaspoon onion salt
1/4 cup oil
1 medium onion, sliced
2 medium red capsicum, sliced
450 g can pineapple pieces
 in syrup

1 teaspoon chicken stock
 powder
1 tablespoon soy sauce
1 tablespoon barbecue sauce

➤ PREHEAT OVEN to moderate 180°C. Tuck chicken wing tips to the underside. Combine cornflour with ginger and onion salt in large bowl. Add chicken and toss to coat; shake off any excess.

1 Heat oil in a large heavy-based pan; add chicken. Cook over medium-high heat 5 minutes or until just golden but not cooked through, turning once. Remove from pan and drain on paper towels.

2 Add onion and capsicum to pan. Stir over medium heat 5 minutes or until soft. Stir in pineapple with syrup, stock and sauces; bring to the boil. Remove from heat.

3 Arrange chicken over the base of a shallow baking dish. Pour sauce and vegetables over chicken. Bake, uncovered, 15 minutes or until chicken is tender and cooked through, turning once during cooking. Serve immediately with steamed rice and a green vegetable.

COOK'S FILE

Storage time: Cook this dish just before serving

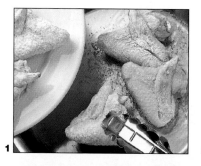

GREEN CHICKEN CURRY

Preparation time: 10 minutes
Total cooking time: 45 minutes
Serves 4

8 (1.5 kg) chicken thigh cutlets
2 tablespoons peanut oil
3 cloves garlic, crushed
3 green chillies, finely chopped
1 tablespoon grated ginger
3 spring onions, finely chopped
3 curry leaves
1/2 teaspoon ground coriander
1/2 teaspoon ground cumin
1 cup water
150 g can coconut cream
1/2 cup finely chopped fresh
 coriander

3 teaspoons Thai fish sauce
 (nam pla)
2 medium tomatoes, seeded,
 chopped
salt, to taste

➤ TRIM CHICKEN of excess fat and sinew.

1 Heat oil in medium heavy-based pan; add garlic, chillies, ginger, spring onions and curry leaves. Stir over medium heat 1 minute.

2 Add chicken and spices to pan. Cook over medium heat 5 minutes each side, turning once. Add water to pan, bring to boil. Reduce heat and simmer gently, covered, for 15 minutes, turning chicken once.

3 Stir in coconut cream, coriander, fish sauce, tomato and salt. Simmer,

uncovered, for 10 minutes or until the chicken is tender and cooked through. Serve with steamed rice.

COOK'S FILE

Storage: This dish can be made one day ahead. Store in refrigerator.
Hints: Fish sauce can be replaced with 3 teaspoons soy sauce. However, for authentic Thai flavour fish sauce should be used. It is available from Asian food stores and supermarkets.
Curry leaves are small glossy curry-flavoured leaves used like bay leaves. They are usually sold dried, but are also available fresh. There is no substitute.
Do not cover the pan after adding coconut cream or milk to a dish as the milk may separate.

*Pineapple and Capsicum Chicken (top)
and Green Chicken Curry.*

CHICKEN PAPRIKA WITH HERB DUMPLINGS

Preparation time: 20 minutes
Total cooking time: 1 hour 10 minutes
Serves 4–6

1.6 kg chicken
2 tablespoons oil
1 large onion, chopped
1 clove garlic, crushed
1 teaspoon sweet paprika
1 teaspoon dried thyme
2 tablespoon plain flour
1/2 cup chicken stock (see page 11)
410 g can peeled tomatoes, crushed
salt and freshly ground black pepper, to taste
2 medium carrots, sliced

Herb Dumplings
1 cup self-raising flour
20 g butter
2 teaspoons finely chopped fresh parsley
2 teaspoons finely chopped fresh chives
1/2 teaspoon dried mixed herbs
1/3 cup buttermilk

➤ PREHEAT OVEN to moderate 180°C. Remove giblets and any large deposits of fat from chicken. Wipe and pat dry with paper towels. Using poultry shears, cut into 10 portions.
1 Heat oil in a heavy-based frying pan. Cook the chicken pieces in batches over medium-high heat until browned, then place in a deep 3-litre capacity ovenproof casserole. Add onion and garlic to frying pan and cook, stirring, until soft; reduce heat to low. Add paprika, thyme and flour; cook, stirring, for 2 minutes. Add stock gradually, stirring constantly. Add tomatoes, season to taste, mix well. Pour mixture over chicken. Place carrots around chicken. Cover dish and bake for 30 minutes.
2 To make Herb Dumplings: Sift flour into a medium mixing bowl. Add chopped butter. Using fingertips, rub butter into flour for 3 minutes or until mixture is fine and crumbly. Stir in herbs. Add almost all the liquid and mix to a soft dough, adding more liquid if necessary.

3 Turn onto a floured surface and knead for 1 minute or until smooth. Divide dough into eight equal portions, and roll into rough balls.
4 Remove casserole from oven. Arrange dumplings on top. Bake, uncovered, a further 20 minutes. Serve immediately.

COOK'S FILE

Storage time: This dish can be made to the end of Step 1 up to two days ahead. Reheat before adding dumplings and bake as directed.

CHICKEN PAELLA

Preparation time: 10 minutes
Total cooking time: 30 minutes
Serves 4

8 (856 g) chicken drumsticks
2 tablespoons olive oil
60 g thin spicy sausage, sliced diagonally
1 large onion, sliced
2 cloves garlic, crushed
1/2 teaspoon tumeric
1 cup short-grain rice
1 1/2 cups chicken stock (see page 11)

1 medium red capsicum, cut into short, thin strips
150 g green beans, cut into 3 cm lengths
150 g broccoli, cut into small florets
salt and freshly ground black pepper, to taste
8 medium green prawns, peeled and deveined

➤ TRIM CHICKEN of excess fat and sinew.

1 Heat oil in a large heavy-based pan. Cook chicken in batches over a medium-high heat until browned; remove from pan; drain. Fry sausage for 1 minute or until just browned.

Add onion and garlic to pan and cook, stirring, for 1 minute.

2 Add turmeric and rice to pan and cook 1 minute until rice is coated with oil. Add stock and vegetables, season to taste and stir to combine.

3 Bring to boil; reduce heat to low. Place chicken on rice. Simmer, covered, 15 minutes or until liquid is absorbed and rice is tender. Check occasionally that rice is not catching on pan bottom but do not uncover for too long. Add prawns for last 5 minutes of cooking. Serve hot.

COOK'S FILE

Storage time: Cook this dish just before serving.

CRISPY TOMATO AND ONION CHICKEN

Preparation time: 20 minutes
Total cooking time: 30 minutes
Serves 4

1.25 kg chicken pieces
40 g packet French onion
   soup mix
40 g packet tomato soup mix
2 medium onions

2 medium carrots
2 medium zucchini
freshly ground black pepper, to
   taste

➤ PREHEAT OVEN to moderately hot 210°C/190°C gas. Trim chicken of excess fat and sinew. Wipe chicken and pat dry with paper towels.

1 Combine soup mixes in a medium mixing bowl. Coat chicken pieces in soup mixture. Shake off excess.

2 Chop onions, carrot and zucchini into 1 cm cubes. Place vegetables in a single layer in a large baking dish. Add pepper to taste.

3 Sit chicken pieces on top of vegetables. Bake 30 minutes or until chicken is browned. Serve immediately.

COOK'S FILE

Storage time: Cook this dish just before serving.

Variation: Add 1 teaspoon each of ground cumin, sweet paprika and garlic powder to soup mixtures.

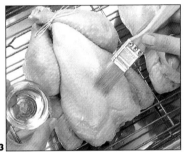

ROAST CHICKEN WITH BACON AND SAGE STUFFING

Preparation time: 15 minutes
Total cooking time: 55 minutes
Serves 6

2 x 1 kg chickens
1 tablespoon oil
2 rashers bacon
1 small onion, finely chopped
1 tablespoon chopped fresh sage
1½ cups fresh breadcrumbs
1 egg, lightly beaten
salt and freshly ground black pepper, to taste

1 tablespoon oil, extra
2 rashers bacon, extra

➤ PREHEAT OVEN to moderate 180°C.

1 Remove giblets and any large fat deposits from chicken. Wipe over and dry with paper towels.

2 Heat oil in a small heavy-based pan. Add bacon and onion and cook until onion is soft and bacon is just starting to brown. Transfer to a mixing bowl and allow to cool. Add sage, breadcrumbs and egg to onion mixture, season to taste and mix to combine. Spoon the stuffing into cavity of the chickens.

3 Fold wings back behind chickens. Tie legs together to keep in place. Place chickens in a large baking dish, making sure they are not touching, and brush with oil.

4 Cut bacon into thin strips and lay across chicken breasts. Brush bacon with oil. Bake for 45 minutes, or until juices run clear when thigh is pierced with a skewer. Serve immediately, with seasonal vegetables.

COOK'S FILE

Storage time: Cook this dish just before serving. The stuffing can be made up to two hours ahead. Stuff chickens immediately before baking.

APRICOT CHICKEN

Preparation time: 15 minutes
Total cooking time: 30 minutes
Serves 6

1.5 kg chicken thigh fillets
1 tablespoon oil
120 g dried apricots
1¹/2 cups apricot nectar
¹/2 cup chicken stock (see
   page 11)
40 g packet French onion
   soup mix
salt and freshly ground black
   pepper, to taste
1 tablespoon finely chopped
   fresh parsley

➤ TRIM CHICKEN of excess fat and sinew.

1 Cut chicken into 3 cm squares. Heat oil in a large heavy-based pan. Cook chicken in batches over medium-high heat until browned; remove from heat and drain on paper towels.

2 Slice dried apricots into strips. Return chicken to pan with apricots, apricot nectar, stock and soup mix; season to taste, mix well. Bring to boil, reduce heat and simmer, covered, 20 minutes, stirring occasionally until chicken is tender and cooked through and sauce is slightly thickened.

3 Remove pan from heat. Stir in parsley. Serve hot with steamed green vegetables and crusty bread.

COOK'S FILE

Storage time: Apricot Chicken can be made up to two days ahead. Cool quickly, and refrigerate until ready to serve. Reheat gently.

Variations: Replace dried apricots and apricot nectar with a large can of apricots in heavy syrup, if liked.

Any cut of chicken can be used in this recipe. Increase cooking times for larger pieces.

1

2

3

CHICKEN CACCIATORE

Preparation time: 15 minutes
Total cooking time: 55 minutes
Serves 6

120 g button mushrooms
1 medium onion
12 (1.3 kg) chicken drumsticks
1 tablespoon oil
1 clove garlic, crushed
410 g can tomatoes,
    puréed

½ cup white wine
½ cup chicken stock (see
    page 11)
1 teaspoon dried oregano
1 teaspoon dried thyme
salt and freshly ground black
    pepper, to taste

➤ PREHEAT OVEN to moderate 180°C.

1 Cut the mushrooms in quarters. Finely chop onion.

2 Heat oil in a heavy-based frying pan. Cook drumsticks in small batches over medium-high heat until well browned; transfer to a large oven-proof casserole dish.

3 Place onion and garlic in frying pan; cook over medium heat until golden. Spread over chicken. Add remaining ingredients to pan. Season to taste. Bring to boil, reduce heat and simmer 10 minutes. Pour over chicken. Bake, covered, 35 minutes or until chicken is very tender. Serve with spiral or other small pasta.

COOK'S FILE

Storage time: This dish can be made up to two days ahead.

BARBECUES AND GRILLS

CHICKEN BURGERS WITH GRAINY MUSTARD CREAM

Preparation time: 12 minutes
+ 20 minutes standing
Total cooking time: 10 minutes
Makes 6

500 g chicken mince
2/3 cup packaged breadcrumbs
1 tablespoon mild curry
    powder
2 tablespoons mango chutney
2 tablespoons finely chopped
    continental parsley
1 egg, lightly beaten
salt and freshly ground black
    pepper, to taste

Grainy Mustard Cream
1/4 cup sour cream
1 tablespoon seeded mustard
1 tablespoon mango chutney
1/4 cup olive oil

➤ PLACE MINCE, breadcrumbs, curry powder, chutney, parsley, egg, salt and pepper into mixing bowl.
1 Using hands, press the mixture together until ingredients are well combined. Cover mixture with plastic wrap and stand 20 minutes.
2 Divide mixture into six equal portions. Shape each portion into a patty with lightly oiled hands and flatten slightly. Place the patties onto a lightly oiled grill or flat plate. Cook over medium-high heat for 5 minutes each side or until the burgers are well browned and cooked through, turning once. Serve hot with Grainy Mustard Cream.
3 To make Grainy Mustard Cream: Place cream, mustard and chutney in small bowl. Using a wire whisk, stir to combine. Add oil a few drops at a time, beating thoroughly until all the oil has been added.

COOK'S FILE

Storage time: Cook this dish just before serving. Uncooked patties can be frozen for up to four weeks. Stack patties and place a layer of plastic wrap between each. Seal in an airtight container.
Hint: For a casual lunch, offer a basket of bread rolls, and plates of red onion rings, torn lettuce leaves, sliced tomato and any other ingredients you like and let guests construct their own burgers. Serve Grainy Mustard Cream in a separate bowl. Or, serve Chicken Burgers on a plate, topped with Grainy Mustard Cream, with a salad and baked potatoes.
Variation: Add a tang to this recipe by using hot curry powder or curry paste instead of mild, or adding cayenne pepper to taste.

BACON-WRAPPED CHICKEN PARCELS

Preparation time: 10 minutes
Total cooking time: 10 minutes
Serves 3

6 (750 g) chicken breast fillets
2 tablespoons olive oil
2 tablespoons lime juice
1/4 teaspoon ground coriander
salt and freshly ground black
**   pepper, to taste**

1/3 cup fruit chutney
1/4 cup chopped pecan nuts
6 rashers bacon

➤ TRIM CHICKEN of excess fat and sinew and remove skin. Place oil, juice, coriander, salt and pepper in small bowl and mix well.

1 Using a sharp knife, cut a pocket in the thickest section of each fillet. Combine chutney and nuts together in a small bowl. Spoon 1 tablespoon of chutney mixture into each chicken breast pocket.

2 Turn tapered end of fillets to underside. Wrap a bacon rasher firm-ly around each fillet to enclose filling. Secure bacon with a toothpick.

3 Place chicken parcels onto lightly oiled grill or flat plate. Cook over medium heat 5 minutes each side or until well browned and cooked through, turning once.

4 Brush parcels with the lime juice mixture several times during cooking. Pour any leftover mixture over cooked chicken just before serving.

COOK'S FILE

Storage time: Cook this dish just before serving. Parcels can be assembled up to two hours beforehand.

CRUNCHY HERB AND PARMESAN CHICKEN

Preparation time: 15 minutes
Total cooking time: 13 minutes
Serves 4

100 g butter
1 tablespoon finely chopped chives
1 tablespoon finely chopped fresh basil
1 tablespoon finely chopped fresh mint
3 teaspoons chopped fresh dill
1 teaspoon finely grated lemon rind
2 teaspoons lemon juice
2 tablespoons grated parmesan cheese
salt and freshly ground black pepper, to taste
8 (750 g) chicken thighs
2 tablespoons grated parmesan cheese, extra

➤ LINE AN OVEN tray with aluminium foil. Brush foil with melted butter.

1 Using electric beaters, beat butter until light and creamy. Add herbs, lemon rind and juice and parmesan and beat until well combined.

2 Loosen the skin from one end of each thigh. Spread herb butter underneath skin of each thigh. Secure skin to flesh with toothpicks.

3 Place thighs on prepared tray; grill under medium heat 6 minutes on each side, or until cooked through. Place thighs skin-side up on tray. Sprinkle with extra parmesan cheese and grill 1 minute or until cheese is melted and lightly browned. Discard toothpicks. Serve immediately.

COOK'S FILE

Storage time: Chicken can be prepared up to Step 3 a day ahead. Refrigerate until ready to use. Cook just before serving.

Hint: To prevent skin burning, grill chicken 10 cm from heat.

TANDOORI CHICKEN ON SKEWERS

Preparation time: 15 minutes
+ 3 hours marinating
Total cooking time: 8 minutes
Makes about 16

6 (750 g) single chicken breast
  fillets
2 teaspoons turmeric
1 teaspoon sweet paprika
1 teaspoon garam masala
1/2 teaspoon ground cardamom
1 teaspoon ground coriander
1 small onion, grated
1 clove garlic, crushed

2 teaspoons lemon juice
2 teaspoons sugar
salt, to taste
1 cup plain yoghurt
red food colouring (optional)

➤ SOAK BAMBOO SKEWERS for several hours in water. Trim chicken of excess fat and sinew.

1 Combine turmeric, paprika, garam masala, cardamom, coriander, onion, garlic, lemon juice, sugar, salt and yoghurt in a large mixing bowl; mix until well combined, stirring in a few drops of red food colouring if desired.

2 Cut chicken fillets into long strips, 2 cm wide. Add to marinade; mix until chicken is well coated. Store,

covered with plastic wrap, in the refrigerator for 3 hours or overnight, stirring occasionally. Drain and reserve marinade.

3 Thread chicken onto skewers. Place skewers on lightly greased grill or flat plate. Cook over medium/high heat 8 minutes or until tender and well browned, turning often and brushing with reserved marinade several times during cooking.

COOK'S FILE

Storage time: Cook this dish just before serving.

Variation: Drumsticks can be marinated in the tandoori mixture. Cook whole, as directed, turning often.

CHILLI CHICKEN WITH SALSA

Preparation time: 10 minutes
+ 3 hours marinating
Total cooking time: 10 minutes
Serves 4

8 (880 g) chicken thigh cutlets
1/2 cup lemon juice
1/2 teaspoon bottled crushed
  chilli
2 tablespoons oil
2 teaspoons sesame oil
2 tablespoons soy sauce
2 tablespoons honey
1 clove garlic, crushed
2 spring onions, chopped

2 tablespoons finely chopped
  fresh coriander
salt, to taste

Salsa
1 small green cucumber,
  chopped
1 small red onion, finely
  chopped
1 medium tomato, chopped
2 tablespoons olive oil
1 tablespoon white wine
  vinegar
1/4 teaspoon caster sugar
1/4 cup fresh coriander leaves

➤ TRIM CHICKEN of excess fat and sinew.

1 Combine juice, chilli, oils, soy sauce,

honey, garlic, spring onions, coriander and salt in a large bowl; mix well. Add chicken, stir to combine. Cover with plastic wrap. Refrigerate, 3 hours or overnight, stirring occasionally.

2 Drain chicken; reserve marinade. Place chicken on lightly oiled grill or flat plate. Cook over medium heat for 5 minutes each side or until tender and cooked through. Brush with reserved marinade in the last minutes of cooking. Serve hot with Salsa.

3 To make Salsa: Combine all ingredients in a bowl and mix well.

COOK'S FILE

Storage time: Cook this dish just before serving. Salsa can be made a day ahead. Serve at room temperature.

*Tandoori Chicken on Skewers (top) and
Chilli Chicken with Salsa.*

GARLIC CHICKEN KEBABS WITH TOMATO AND MUSHROOM SALAD

Preparation time: 20 minutes
Total cooking time: 12 minutes
Makes 12

6 (750 g) chicken thigh fillets
1 medium red capsicum, cut
   into 3 cm pieces
1 medium green capsicum, cut
   into 3 cm pieces
1 large red onion, cut into
   12 wedges
1/2 cup olive oil
2 cloves garlic, crushed
1 tablespoon chopped fresh
   chives
1 tablespoon chopped fresh
   mint
1 tablespoon chopped fresh
   thyme
1/2 teaspoon seasoned
   pepper

Tomato and Mushroom Salad
250 g cherry tomatoes
150 g button mushrooms,
   quartered
1 clove garlic, crushed
1/4 cup olive oil
1 tablespoon white wine
   vinegar
salt, to taste
1 tablespoon chopped fresh
   chives
1 tablespoon chopped fresh
   mint
1 tablespoon chopped fresh
   thyme

➤ SOAK BAMBOO SKEWERS in
water for several hours.

1 Trim chicken of excess fat and
sinew. Cut chicken into 3 cm cubes.
2 Thread chicken, capsicum and
onion alternately onto skewers.
Combine oil, garlic, herbs and pepper
in a small bowl.
3 Place kebabs on lightly oiled grill.
Cook skewers under medium-high
heat 6 minutes each side or until
cooked through, brushing with herb
mixture several times during cooking. Serve hot with Tomato and
Mushroom Salad.
**To make Tomato and Mush-
room Salad:** Combine all ingredients in medium bowl; mix well.

COOK'S FILE

Storage time: Kebabs can be
assembled a day ahead. Refrigerate,
covered, until needed. Cook just
before serving. Salad can be made
several hours ahead.

CURRY, COCONUT AND LIME DRUMSTICKS

Preparation time: 10 minutes
+ 3 hours marinating
Total cooking time: 16 minutes
Serves 4

8 (856 g) chicken drumsticks
6 teaspoons curry paste
1 teaspoon grated lime rind
2 tablespoons lime juice
2/3 cup coconut cream
3 teaspoons honey
salt, to taste
2 tablespoons desiccated
  coconut
3 teaspoons grated lime rind,
  extra

➤ LINE AN OVEN tray with foil. Brush with melted butter or oil.

1 Secure skin of drumsticks to joint with toothpicks.

2 Make three deep cuts into the thickest section of the drumstick. Combine curry paste, lime rind and juice, coconut cream and honey in a large bowl. Add chicken and mix to coat well. Store, covered, in refrigerator 3 hours or overnight, stirring occasionally. Drain: reserve marinade.

3 Place drumsticks on prepared tray. Grill 8 minutes each side or until cooked through, brushing occasionally with reserved marinade. Discard toothpicks.

4 Combine the coconut and lime rind, sprinkle over chicken. Serve hot.

COOK'S FILE

Storage time: Cook this dish just before serving.

GRILLED CHICKEN WINGS

Preparation time: 10 minutes
+ 2 hours marinating
Total cooking time: 12 minutes
Serves 4

12 (1.2 kg) chicken wings
2 tablespoons soy sauce
2 tablespoons hoi sin sauce
1/3 cup tomato sauce
1 tablespoon honey
1 tablespoon soft brown sugar
1 tablespoon cider vinegar
2 cloves garlic, crushed

1/4 teaspoon Chinese five-spice
  powder
salt, to taste
2 teaspoons sesame oil

➤ WIPE CHICKEN wings and pat
dry with paper towels.
1 Tuck wing tips to underside.
Combine all the remaining ingredients in a large bowl; mix well.
2 Add wings and mix well to coat.
Store, covered with plastic wrap, in
refrigerator 2 hours or overnight,
turning occasionally. Drain chicken
and reserve marinade.
3 Preheat grill. Place wings on a
cold, lightly-oiled tray. Cook chicken

under medium-high heat, 6 minutes on
each side or until tender and cooked
through, brushing with reserved marinade several times during cooking.
Serve hot or cold as an appetiser.

COOK'S FILE

Storage time: Grilled Chicken
Wings can be made up to one day
ahead. Store, covered, in the refrigerator. Reheat in a moderate 180°C
oven if desired, or in a microwave on
Medium/High for 2–3 minutes.
Note: Hoi sin sauce, sesame oil and
Chinese five-spice powder are available from supermarkets and Asian
food suppliers.

GINGER-CHILLI DRUMSTICKS WITH CUCUMBER YOGHURT

Preparation time: 10 minutes
+ 3 hours marinating
Total cooking time: 16 minutes
Serves 6

12 (1.3 kg) drumsticks
1 tablespoon grated fresh
  ginger
2 teaspoons bottled crushed
  chilli
1/4 teaspoon ground turmeric
1 teaspoon lemon juice
1 teaspoon grated lemon rind
1 1/2 teaspoons soft brown sugar
1 cup plain yoghurt

Cucumber Yoghurt
1 cup plain yoghurt
1 teaspoon bottled crushed
  chilli
1 Lebanese cucumber, finely
  chopped
salt, to taste
1/2 teaspoon caster sugar

➤ LINE AN OVEN TRAY with foil.
Lightly brush tray with melted butter
or oil.
1 Combine ginger, chilli, turmeric,
lemon juice and rind, sugar and
yoghurt in a large bowl; mix well.
Add chicken, stir well to coat with
marinade. Store, covered with plastic
wrap, in refrigerator 3 hours or
overnight, stirring occasionally.
Drain chicken; reserve marinade.

2 Place drumsticks on prepared tray
and grill, brushing frequently with
marinade, under medium heat 8 minutes on each side or until cooked
through. Serve hot or cold with
Cucumber Yoghurt.
3 To make Cucumber Yoghurt:
Combine all ingredients in small
bowl and mix well.

COOK'S FILE

Storage time: Drumsticks can be
cooked up to one day ahead. Store,
covered, in refrigerator. Chilli
Cucumber Yoghurt can be made up to
one day ahead. Store in refrigerator.
Variation: For a cooler-flavoured
sauce, omit chilli from the Cucumber
Yoghurt and replace with 1 teaspoon
chopped fresh mint.

Chinese Barbecued Wings (top) and
Ginger-Chilli Drumsticks with Cucumber Yoghurt.

CHICKEN SATAY WITH PEANUT SAUCE

Preparation time: 30 minutes
+ 2 hours marinating
Total cooking time: 10 minutes
Makes 12

1 kg chicken thigh fillets
1/4 cup soy sauce
1 tablespoon honey
2 tablespoons oil

Peanut Sauce
1 tablespoon oil
2 teaspoons dried onion
   flakes
3/4 cup crunchy peanut butter
1/2 cup coconut cream
1 tablespoon soy sauce
2 tablespoons sweet chilli sauce

1/2 cup water
salt, to taste

➤ TRIM CHICKEN of excess fat and sinew. Soak bamboo skewers in water for several hours.

1 Cut chicken into 2 cm strips. Thread onto skewers. Place in a shallow glass or ceramic dish. Combine soy sauce, honey and oil and pour over chicken. Refrigerate, covered with plastic wrap, for 2 hours, turning occasionally.

2 To make Peanut Sauce: Heat oil in a small heavy-based pan. Add onion flakes and cook over a low heat for 30 seconds, taking care not to let them burn. Add peanut butter, coconut cream, soy sauce, sweet chilli sauce, water and salt; stir until well combined. Cook gently until heated through.

3 Drain chicken and reserve marinade. Place satay sticks on a lightly greased grill or flat plate. Cook over medium-high heat for about 8 minutes, turning often and brushing occasionally with reserved marinade. Serve immediately with Peanut Sauce and crunchy fried noodles.

COOK'S FILE

Storage time: Chicken Satay can be assembled and refrigerated in marinade for up to eight hours. Cook just before serving. Peanut sauce can be made up to eight hours ahead. Store in refrigerator; thin down with a little extra water when reheating.
Hint: Satay sticks make great party nibbles. Buy very small skewers, or cut larger ones in half and place only a couple of bites of meat on each. Serve with Peanut Sauce as a dip.

1

2

3

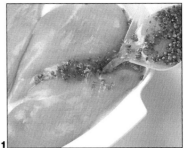

CORIANDER CHICKEN WITH TABOULI

Preparation time: 30 minutes
+ 1 hour marinating
Total cooking time: 14 minutes
Serves 4

4 (500 g) chicken breast fillets
1/3 cup lime juice
1 tablespoon sesame oil
2 tablespoons crushed
   coriander seeds

Tabouli
1/3 cup burghul or cracked
   wheat
1/3 cup hot water
1 bunch flat leaf parsley
2 spring onions, finely chopped
2 medium tomatoes, chopped
2 tablespoons lemon juice
2 tablespoons olive oil
salt, to taste

➤ TRIM CHICKEN of excess fat and sinew.

1 Place chicken breasts in a shallow, glass or ceramic dish. Combine lime juice, oil and coriander seeds in small bowl, pour over chicken. Place, covered with plastic wrap, in the refrigerator for 1 hour, turning occasionally.

2 To make Tabouli: Combine burghul and hot water in a small bowl. Leave to stand for 10 minutes, or until all the water is absorbed.

3 Cut off and discard thick stems from parsley; wash and dry thoroughly and chop roughly. Combine all ingredients in large bowl; mix well.

4 Drain chicken and reserve marinade. Place chicken breasts on a lightly oiled grill or flat plate. Cook for about 7 minutes each side, brushing occasionally with reserved marinade. Serve with Tabouli.

COOK'S FILE

Storage time: Chicken can be refrigerated in the marinade for up to eight hours. Cook just before serving.
Note: Burghul, or cracked wheat, is available from supermarkets, delicatessens and specialty food stores.

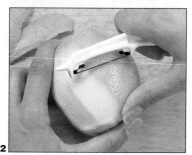

GRILLED GARLIC AND ROSEMARY MARYLANDS

Preparation time: 10 minutes
 + 3 hours marinating
Total cooking time: 20 minutes
Serves 4

4 (1.7 kg) chicken maryland
  pieces
1 orange
1/2 cup orange juice
2/3 cup olive oil
3 cloves garlic, crushed
2 tablespoons chopped fresh
  rosemary
1 tablespoon chopped fresh
  thyme
1 teaspoon Dijon mustard
salt, to taste

➤ TRIM CHICKEN of excess fat and sinew. Line an oven tray with foil. Brush foil with melted butter or oil.
1 Using a sharp knife, make 3 or 4 deep cuts into the thickest section of the marylands.
2 Using a vegetable peeler, peel long strips from half the orange.
3 Combine orange rind and juice, oil, garlic, rosemary, thyme, mustard and salt in a small bowl. Place marylands in a large shallow dish and pour garlic-herb mixture over. Cover with plastic wrap, refrigerate 3 hours or overnight, turning occasionally. Drain chicken and reserve marinade.
4 Place marylands onto the prepared oven tray. Grill under medium heat 10 minutes each side or until tender and cooked through, brushing with reserved marinade several times during cooking. Garnish with slices of orange and sprigs of rosemary.

COOK'S FILE

Storage time: Cook this dish just before serving.

CHICKEN WITH ORANGE-CHIVE BUTTER

Preparation time: 20 minutes
+ 2 hours marinating
Total cooking time: 20 minutes
Serves 4

8 (720 g) chicken thighs
1/2 cup orange juice
1 teaspoon ground black pepper
2 teaspoons sesame oil

Orange-chive Butter
100 g butter
1 teaspoon finely grated orange rind
1 tablespoon finely chopped chives

1 tablespoon orange marmalade
salt, to taste

➤ TRIM CHICKEN meat of excess fat and sinew.

1 Place chicken in a shallow glass or ceramic dish. Combine juice, pepper and oil in a small jug and pour over chicken. Cover with plastic wrap and refrigerate for 2 hours, turning occasionally. Drain chicken and reserve marinade. Place chicken on a cold, lightly oiled grill tray and cook under a medium heat for 10 minutes each side, brushing occasionally with reserved marinade. Serve immediately with slices of Orange-chive Butter.

2 To make Orange-chive Butter: Allow butter to soften slightly at room temperature. Place in a small mixing bowl and beat with a wooden spoon for 1 minute until creamy. Add the remaining ingredients and mix until well combined.

3 Place butter on a sheet of plastic wrap and form into a log shape. Roll up tightly and refrigerate until required. Serve sliced.

COOK'S FILE

Storage: Chicken can be refrigerated in marinade up to eight hours. Cook just before serving. Orange-chive Butter can be stored up to two days in the refrigerator, or two weeks in the freezer. Allow frozen butter to thaw completely before slicing and serving.

Hint: Chicken is cooked if juices run clear when a skewer is inserted into thickest part of the meat.

SOUTHERN-STYLE DRUMSTICKS

Preparation time: 15 minutes
  + 4 hours marinating
Total cooking time: 25 minutes
Serves 4

8 (856 g) drumsticks
1/2 cup buttermilk
2 cloves garlic, crushed
1 teaspoon ground cumin
1/4 teaspoon cayenne pepper
1/4 teaspoon salt
1/4 teaspoon black pepper

2 cobs of corn, halved
20 g butter
4 drops Tabasco sauce

➤ TRIM CHICKEN of excess fat and sinew.

1 Place drumsticks in a shallow glass or ceramic dish. Combine buttermilk, garlic, cumin, cayenne pepper, salt and black pepper, pour over chicken. Cover with plastic wrap and refrigerate for 4 hours, turning occasionally. Drain chicken.

2 Place drumsticks on a lightly oiled grill or flat plate. Grill on medium heat for 25 minutes, turning occasion-

ally, until chicken is tender and cooked through. Serve immediately, with cooked corn cobs.

3 Cook corn in a large pan of boiling water for 10 minutes. Drain and place on individual pieces of aluminium foil. Melt butter; add Tabasco and brush liberally onto corn. Wrap in foil; place on barbecue for 10 minutes, turning occasionally.

COOK'S FILE

Storage: Chicken can be refrigerated in marinade overnight. Cook just before serving. Corn is best cooked just before serving.

1

3

GRILLED CHICKEN WITH FETA

Preparation time: 15 minutes
+ 4 hours marinating
Total cooking time: 20 minutes
Serves 6

6 (750 g) chicken breast
   fillets
1/2 cup plain yoghurt
2 tablespoons olive oil
2 tablespoons lemon juice
1/2 teaspoon ground oregano
1/4 teaspoon black pepper

salt, to taste
75 g feta cheese

➤ TRIM CHICKEN of excess fat and sinew.
1 Place chicken in a shallow glass or ceramic dish. Combine yoghurt, oil, lemon juice, oregano and pepper in small bowl and pour over chicken. Mix to combine. Refrigerate, covered with plastic wrap, for 4 hours, turning occasionally. Drain and reserve marinade.
2 Place chicken on cold, lightly oiled grill tray. Cook under medium heat for 7 minutes each side, or until ten-

der and cooked through, brushing with reserved marinade occasionally.
3 Slice feta thinly, and lay pieces across breast. Replace under heat for 2 minutes or until cheese starts to bubble slightly. Serve immediately, with a salad of tomato, olives, capsicum, onion rings and lettuce or grilled eggplant and bread rolls.

COOK'S FILE

Storage: Chicken can be refrigerated in marinade for up to eight hours. Cook just before serving.
Variation: Use goat cheese in place of feta in this recipe.

CHICKEN TERIYAKI

Preparation time: 20 minutes
  + 2 hours marinating
Total cooking time: 6 minutes
Makes 12

750 g chicken tenderloins
¼ cup soy sauce
2 tablespoons mirin (optional)
2 tablespoons sherry
2 tablespoons soft brown sugar
2 teaspoons grated fresh ginger
1 medium red capsicum, cut
    into 2 cm squares
4 spring onions, cut into 3 cm
    lengths
salt, to taste
2 tablespoons oil

➤ TRIM CHICKEN of excess fat and sinew. Soak bamboo skewers in water to prevent burning.

1 Place chicken in a shallow glass or ceramic dish. Combine soy sauce, mirin, sherry, brown sugar and ginger. Stir to dissolve sugar; pour over chicken. Cover and refrigerate for up to 2 hours, turning occasionally. Drain and cut tenderloins in half.

2 Thread chicken onto skewers alternating with capsicum and spring onion pieces.

3 Brush kebabs with oil and place on a lightly oiled grill or flat plate. Cook over medium-high heat 6 minutes or until tender, turning and brushing with oil occasionally. Serve immediately, with steamed rice or Japanese-style egg noodles and stir-fried or grilled vegetables.

COOK'S FILE

Storage: Chicken Teriyaki can be assembled and refrigerated in marinade for up to 4 hours. Cook just before serving.
Variation: Use chicken thigh fillets, cut into strips, instead of tenderloins.

1

2

3

BARBECUED HONEY CHICKEN WINGS

Preparation time: 10 minutes
Total cooking time: 14 minutes
Serves 4

12 (1.2 kg) chicken wings
¼ cup soy sauce
1 clove garlic, crushed
2 tablespoons sherry
2 tablespoons oil
2 tablespoons honey

➤ WIPE AND PAT DRY chicken wings with paper towels. Tuck wing tips to underside.

1 Place wings in a shallow glass or ceramic dish. Combine soy sauce, garlic, sherry and oil in small jug and pour over chicken.

2 Place, covered with plastic wrap, in the refrigerator for 2 hours, turning occasionally. Drain chicken and place on a lightly oiled grill or flat plate. Place the honey in a small heatproof cup or jug on a cool part of the grill to warm and thin down a lit-

tle. Cook chicken wings for 12 minutes or until tender and cooked through, turning occasionally.

3 Brush wings with honey and cook 2 minutes more. Serve immediately.

COOK'S FILE

Storage: Barbecued Honey Chicken Wings can be refrigerated in marinade for up to eight hours. Cook just before serving.

Variation: Substitute apricot jam for the honey, if desired. Add bottled crushed chilli to taste, if liked.

SNACKS, SOUPS & SALADS

CHICKEN AND LEEK PASTRIES

Preparation time: 40 minutes
Total cooking time: 38 minutes
Makes 20

1 tablespoon oil
3 (330 g) chicken thigh fillets
30 g butter
2 medium leeks, finely sliced
1 bacon rasher, finely chopped
1 clove garlic, crushed
1/4 cup dry white wine
1/4 cup cream
2 teaspoons seeded mustard
salt and freshly ground black
    pepper, to taste
1/4 cup grated parmesan cheese
10 sheets filo pastry
80 g butter, melted

➤ PREHEAT OVEN to moderate 180°C. Brush an oven tray with melted butter or oil.
1 Heat oil in a heavy-based frying pan. Cook chicken 5 minutes on each side, or until browned and tender. Remove from pan and drain on paper towels. Cool; chop chicken finely.

2 Heat butter in a large heavy-based pan. Add leek, bacon and garlic, cook 3–4 minutes or until leek is soft and bacon crisp. Add chicken, wine, cream and mustard. Cook, stirring constantly, 4 minutes or until thickened. Remove from heat, season, and stir in parmesan cheese; cool slightly.
3 Lay a sheet of filo pastry on a flat work surface. Brush sheet with melted butter. Top with another sheet and brush with butter. Cut the pastry evenly lengthways into four pieces. Place 1 tablespoon of chicken mixture at one end of each length. Fold end diagonally over filling. Continue folding to end of length, forming a triangle. Repeat with remaining lengths of filo and filling. Place on prepared oven tray and brush triangles with butter. Repeat with remaining pastry, butter and chicken mixture. Bake 25 minutes, or until pastry is golden brown and filling hot.

COOK'S FILE

Storage time: Uncooked pastries can be kept overnight in the refrigerator. To freeze, seal in an airtight container for up to two months. Cook just before serving.

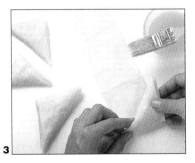

Chicken and Leek Pastries.

CHICKEN PARCELS WITH PLUM SAUCE

Preparation time: 20 minutes
Total cooking time: 15 minutes
Makes about 28

150 g chicken mince
1/4 cup finely grated carrot
2 spring onions, finely
    chopped
1 tablespoon finely chopped
    fresh coriander
1 teaspoon finely grated
    ginger
1 clove garlic, crushed
1 tablespoon soy sauce
1/2 teaspoon sugar
salt, to taste
1 teaspoon sesame oil
200 g round wonton
    wrappers
oil for deep-frying

Plum sauce
1 cup bottled plum sauce
1 tablespoon soy sauce

➤ PLACE CHICKEN MINCE in food processor bowl. Using the pulse action, press button for 20 seconds or until mixture is smooth.

1 Combine chicken mince, carrot, spring onions, coriander, ginger, garlic, soy sauce, sugar, salt and sesame oil in a medium bowl; mix well.

2 Place 1 1/2 teaspoons of mixture into centre of each wrapper. Brush edges of wrappers with a little water. Bring edges together to form pouches and squeeze gently to secure.

3 Heat oil in a deep, heavy-based pan. Lower pouches into moderately hot oil. Cook in batches over medium heat for 1 minute or until golden, crisp and cooked through. Remove from oil with a slotted spoon, drain on paper towels; keep warm. Serve hot with Plum Sauce.

4 To make Plum Sauce: Combine plum and soy sauces in small pan and stir over medium heat until heated through.

COOK'S FILE

Storage time: Chicken Parcels can be assembled up to Step 3 a day ahead. Refrigerate, covered well in plastic wrap or in an airtight container, to prevent drying out. Cook just before serving.

Note: Wonton wrappers are available from Asian food stores.

SPICY CHICKEN PASTIES

Preparation time: 30 minutes
Total cooking time: 30 minutes
Makes 20

2 tablespoons oil
1 small onion, finely chopped
1 clove garlic, crushed
1/2 teaspoon ground coriander
1/2 teaspoon ground cumin
1/4 teaspoon ground turmeric
1/4 teaspoon chilli powder
300 g chicken mince
1/3 cup frozen peas

1 tablespoon finely chopped
     fresh coriander
salt, to taste
5 sheets ready-rolled puff pastry
1 egg, lightly beaten

➤ PREHEAT OVEN to moderate 180°C. Line an oven tray with foil.

1 Heat oil in a heavy-based frying pan. Add onion and garlic and cook over medium heat for 2 minutes or until onion is soft. Add all the spices and cook, stirring, for 1 minute.

2 Add chicken mince to pan and cook for 10 minutes until almost all liquid has evaporated, stirring occa-

sionally. Stir in peas, coriander and salt to taste. Remove from heat; cool.

3 Using a small plate or saucer as a guide, cut 10 cm circles from pastry with a sharp knife. Place a level tablespoon of mixture in the centre of each circle. Fold over and pleat the edges to seal. Place on prepared tray and brush with beaten egg. Bake for 15 minutes or until golden.

COOK'S FILE

Storage time: Uncooked pasties can be prepared several hours ahead. Store, covered, in the refrigerator. Cook just before serving.

1

2

3

HEARTY CHICKEN NOODLE SOUP

Preparation time: 30 minutes
Total cooking time: 15 minutes
Serves 6

^{1}/2 cup dried Chinese
   mushrooms
150 g fresh Chinese egg
   noodles
^{1}/2 bunch choy sum
1 tablespoon peanut oil
2 tablespoons sesame oil
1 medium onion, chopped
6 cups (1^1/2 L) chicken stock
   (see page 11)
2 tablespoons soy sauce
1 tablespoon thinly shredded
   fresh ginger
1 clove garlic, crushed
4 (500 g) chicken breast fillets,
   thinly sliced
salt, to taste
425 g can baby corn, drained,
   chopped
1 large red capsicum, thinly
   sliced

➤ SOAK MUSHROOMS in boiling water for 20 minutes. Drain and squeeze out excess liquid. Slice finely. Cook noodles in rapidly boiling water until just tender. Rinse; drain well.

1 Cut leaves from stems of choy sum. Cut stems into 4 cm lengths. Cut leaves into 1 cm slices. Heat oils in large heavy-based pan. Add onion and choy sum stems; cook over medium heat, stirring, for 3 minutes or until onion and stems are just tender.

2 Add chicken stock, soy sauce, ginger and garlic to pan. Bring to boil, stirring occasionally. Add chicken. Reduce heat and simmer, stirring, 4 minutes, or until chicken is just cooked through. Season.

3 Add corn, capsicum, choy sum leaves and mushrooms to pan. Bring

to the boil; reduce heat and simmer for 3 minutes or until capsicum and leaves are tender. Do not overcook. To serve, place drained, cooked noodles in the base of each serving bowl. Pour soup over the noodles. Serve immediately.

COOK'S FILE

Storage time: Soup and noodles can be prepared one day in advance. Store separately in airtight containers in the refrigerator. Bring noodles to room temperature and reheat soup gently just before serving.

1

2

3

CHICKEN AND COCONUT MILK SOUP

Preparation time: 30 minutes
Total cooking time: 12 minutes
Serves 8

150 g rice vermicelli
1 lime
4 small fresh red chillies, seeded, chopped
1 medium onion, chopped
2 cloves garlic, crushed
4 thin slices fresh ginger, finely chopped
2 stalks lemongrass root, roughly chopped
1 tablespoon chopped fresh coriander
1 tablespoon peanut oil
3 cups chicken stock (see page 11)
2³/4 cups coconut milk
500 g chicken tenderloin, cut into fine strips
4 spring onions, chopped
150 g fried bean curd or tofu, sliced
1 cup bean sprouts
salt, to taste
3 teaspoons soft brown sugar

➤ POUR BOILING WATER over vermicelli to cover. Stand 5 minutes or until the noodles are tender; drain. Cut into shorter lengths with scissors and set aside.

1 Remove the lime rind with a vegetable peeler. Cut into long, thin strips.
2 Place chillies, onion, garlic, ginger, lemongrass and coriander in a food processor bowl or blender. Using pulse action, process 20 seconds or until the mixture is smooth.
3 Heat oil in a large heavy-based pan. Add chilli mixture; cook 3 minutes until fragrance is released, stirring frequently. Add stock, coconut milk and lime rind and bring to boil. Add chicken and cook, stirring, 4 minutes or until chicken is tender.

4 Add spring onions to soup with bean curd, sprouts, salt and sugar. Stir over medium heat 3 minutes or until spring onions are tender. To serve, divide noodles between serving bowls; pour soup over noodles. Garnish with thinly sliced red chillies and whole coriander leaves, if liked.

COOK'S FILE

Storage time: Soup can be made up to Step 4 one day ahead. Just before serving, cook noodles, reheat soup and add remaining ingredients.

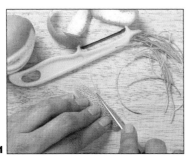

WARM CHICKEN SALAD

Preparation time: 20 minutes
Total cooking time: 25 minutes
Serves 4

2 large red capsicum
6 (660 g) chicken thigh fillets
400 g green beans
1 tablespoon oil
150 g feta cheese
1 mignonette lettuce

Garlic Mustard Vinaigrette
1/2 cup olive oil
1 tablespoon balsamic vinegar
2 tablespoons white wine
    vinegar
1 clove garlic, crushed
1 tablespoon seeded mustard
salt and freshly ground black
    pepper, to taste

➤ CUT CAPSICUM into quarters. Discard seeds and membranes. Place skin-side up on foil-lined oven tray. Brush with oil.

1 Grill capsicum on high heat for 12–15 minutes or until skin is black. Cover with a damp tea-towel until cool. Peel off skins and cut capsicum into 1 cm strips.

2 Trim chicken of excess fat and sinew. Cut chicken into long thin strips. Trim beans and cut into 5 cm lengths. Heat oil in large heavy-based pan. Cook chicken, in small batches, over medium heat for 3 minutes or until browned. Remove from pan; drain on paper towels.

3 Add beans to pan and cook until just tender. Add chicken and capsicum; stir over heat until heated through. Serve warm on a bed of lettuce leaves, topped with crumbled feta cheese. Just before serving, drizzle with Garlic Mustard Vinaigrette.

4 To make Garlic Mustard Vinaigrette: Place all ingredients in a small screw-top jar; shake well.

COOK'S FILE

Storage time: Salad is best made just before serving. Vinaigrette can be made several days ahead. Store in refrigerator. Shake well before use. Refrigerate grilled capsicum in an airtight container up to three days.

Note: Balsamic vinegar is aged wine vinegar, available from supermarkets.

1

2

3

4

CREAM OF CHICKEN AND VEGETABLE SOUP

Preparation time: 20 minutes
Total cooking time: 1 hour 45 minutes
Serves 6

1.1 kg chicken

Stock
6 cups water
1/2 stick celery, chopped
6 peppercorns
1 bay leaf
1 clove garlic, sliced
1 small onion, chopped

Soup
1 medium carrot
1 tablespoon oil
1 medium onion, sliced
200 g button mushrooms, sliced
1/4 cup plain flour
2/3 cup milk
1 cup cream
100 g snow peas, thinly sliced
3 medium tomatoes, peeled, seeded, chopped
1 tablespoon soy sauce
salt and freshly ground black pepper, to taste

➤ WIPE OVER and dry chicken.
1 To make Stock: Using poultry shears, cut chicken into breasts, thighs, legs and wings. Place in a large heavy-based pan with water, celery, peppercorns, bay leaf, garlic and onion. Bring to boil; reduce heat and simmer, covered, for 1¼ hours. Remove from heat; cool slightly. Strain, reserve stock and chicken; discard onion mixture. (You need 5 cups of stock for this recipe).
2 To make Soup: Cut carrot into matchstick strips. Heat oil in a large heavy-based pan; add onion, carrot and mushrooms. Cook, stirring, over low heat until onion is tender, stir in stock and blended flour and milk. Bring to boil. Reduce heat and simmer, stirring, until slightly thickened.
3 Cut reserved chicken into thin strips. Add chicken, cream, snow peas, tomatoes and soy sauce to soup. Stir until heated through. Season to taste. Serve hot.

COOK'S FILE

Storage time: Stock can be made one month ahead and frozen. Soup can be made one day ahead.

1

2

3

4

ITALIAN-STYLE CHICKEN PASTA SALAD

Preparation time: 30 minutes +
    3 hours marinating
Total cooking time: 10 minutes
Serves 6–8

3 (350 g) chicken breast fillets
1/4 cup lemon juice
1 clove garlic, crushed
100 g thinly sliced prosciutto
1 Lebanese cucumber
2 tablespoons seasoned pepper
2 tablespoons olive oil
1¹/2 cups penne pasta, cooked
1/2 cup thinly sliced sun-dried
    tomatoes
1/2 cup pitted black olives,
    halved
1/2 cup halved bottled artichoke
    hearts
1/2 cup parmesan cheese flakes

Creamy Basil Dressing
1/3 cup olive oil
1 tablespoon white wine vinegar
1/4 teaspoon seasoned pepper
1 teaspoon Dijon mustard
3 teaspoons cornflour
1/3 cup water
2/3 cup cream
1/3 cup shredded fresh basil
salt, to taste

➤ REMOVE EXCESS FAT and sinew from chicken. Flatten chicken slightly with a mallet or rolling pin.
1 Place chicken in medium bowl with combined lemon juice and garlic. Cover with plastic wrap, and refrigerate for at least 3 hours or overnight, turning occasionally.
Cut prosciutto into thin strips. Cut cucumber in half lengthways. Cut each half into slices.
2 Drain chicken and coat in seasoned pepper. Heat oil in a large heavy-based frying pan. Cook the chicken for 4 minutes on each side, or until lightly browned and cooked through. Remove from heat. Cool chicken and cut into 2 cm pieces.
3 Combine pasta, chicken pieces, cucumber slices, prosciutto, sun-dried tomatoes, olives and artichoke hearts in a large serving bowl. Pour warm Creamy Basil Dressing over; toss gently to combine. Serve salad warm or cold, sprinkled with parmesan cheese flakes.
4 To make Creamy Basil Dressing: Combine oil, vinegar, seasoned pepper and mustard in a medium pan. Blend cornflour with water in small bowl or jug until smooth. Add to pan. Whisk over medium heat for 2 minutes, or until sauce boils and thickens. Add cream, basil and salt. Stir until heated through.

COOK'S FILE

Storage time: Make dressing just before assembling salad. Chicken and pasta can be cooked a day ahead and stored, covered, in refrigerator.
Hint: Serve this dish with a large round Italian loaf or multi-coloured vegetable bread. In warm weather accompany the salad with a crisp frascati wine, chilled, or a lightly oaked chardonnay.
Variation: Any small size pasta (such as spirals or shells) can be used instead of penne in this dish.

THAI CHICKEN SALAD

Preparation time: 20 minutes
Total cooking time: 5 minutes
Serves 6

1 cos lettuce
4 sprigs fresh coriander
4 sprigs fresh mint
1 small red onion
3 spring onions
2 tablespoons oil
750 g chicken mince
1/3 cup water
1/3 cup lime juice
2 tablespoons soy sauce
2 tablespoons fish sauce
1 tablespoon sweet chilli sauce

2 cloves garlic, crushed
2 teaspoons soft brown sugar
salt, to taste
1 tablespoon chopped fresh
    lemongrass
1/4 cup roasted peanuts
1 tablespoon fresh coriander
    leaves, extra, for garnish
1 tablespoon chopped roasted
    peanuts, extra, for garnish

➤ WASH AND DRY lettuce leaves thoroughly. Arrange on serving platter.

1 Finely chop coriander and mint. Cut the red onion into thin slices. Chop spring onions.

2 Heat oil in a heavy-based frying pan; add mince and water. Cook over medium heat 5 minutes or until cooked through and almost all liquid has evaporated. Break up any lumps as mince cooks; remove from heat.

3 Transfer chicken to a medium bowl. Stir in chopped coriander, mint, onion and spring onions. Combine lime juice, soy, fish and chilli sauces, garlic, brown sugar, salt and lemongrass in a small bowl; mix well. Stir into chicken mixture. Just before serving, stir in peanuts. Serve on prepared lettuce leaves, sprinkled with extra coriander leaves and peanuts.

COOK'S FILE

Storage time: Recipe can be made up to Step 3 a day ahead. Store in an airtight container in the refrigerator. Assemble just before serving.

1

2

3

CURRIED CHICKEN APPLE AND CELERY SALAD

Preparation time: 30 minutes
Total cooking time: 20 minutes
Serves 8

4 (1720 g) chicken marylands
1 cup orange juice
2 cups water
2 medium red apples
2 celery sticks
1 cup (200 g) green seedless grapes
3/4 cup walnuts, roughly chopped

Curry Mayonnaise
60 g butter
1 small onion, finely chopped
3 teaspoons curry powder
1/3 cup mayonnaise
1/2 cup sour cream
1/3 cup cream
2 tablespoons lemon juice
2 teaspoons soft brown sugar
salt, to taste

➤ TRIM CHICKEN of excess fat and sinew.

1 Place chicken in a large heavy-based pan. Add orange juice and water. Cover and bring to the boil. Reduce heat and gently simmer, covered, until chicken is tender. Remove from heat. Drain and cool. Discard bones; cut meat into 2 cm pieces.

2 Cut apples in half, remove cores and cut into 1.5 cm cubes. Slice celery. Combine chicken, apples, celery, grapes and walnuts in a large bowl.

3 To make Curry Mayonnaise: Melt butter in a small pan. Add onion, cook 2 minutes or until onion is soft. Stir in curry powder, cook 30 seconds. Transfer mixture to a small bowl. Add mayonnaise, creams, juice, sugar and salt; mix well. Gently fold through chicken mixture.

COOK'S FILE

Storage time: Salad can be made a day ahead. Store in refrigerator.

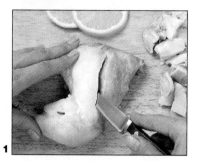

RASPBERRY CHICKEN SALAD

Preparation time: 15 minutes
Total cooking time: 10 minutes
Serves 4

4 (440 g) chicken breast fillets
1 cup white wine
50 g curly endive
1 red coral lettuce
50 g watercress
1/2 cup olive oil
2 tablespoons raspberry vinegar
1/2 teaspoon French mustard

salt and freshly ground black pepper, to taste
200 g punnet raspberries

➤ TRIM CHICKEN of excess fat and sinew.

1 Pour wine into large heavy-based frying pan and add enough water to make the liquid 2–3 cm deep. Cover and bring to the boil. Reduce heat, add chicken to pan, cover and simmer gently 10 minutes or until cooked through. Remove from pan. Drain, cool and cut into slices.

2 Wash and dry endive, lettuce and watercress. Tear into bite-size pieces, discarding thicker stems of watercress. Place into a large mixing bowl.

3 Place olive oil, vinegar, mustard and seasonings in a small screw-top jar and shake well. Pour one-third of the dressing over leaves and toss lightly to combine. Place 1/3 cup of the raspberries and the remaining dressing in food processor bowl. Using the pulse action, process for 10 seconds or until smooth. Arrange salad leaves on serving plates, top with chicken slices and remaining raspberries. Drizzle with raspberry dressing and serve immediately.

COOK'S FILE

Storage: Chicken may be poached up to one day ahead. Refrigerate, covered with plastic wrap, until required.

Curried Chicken, Apple and Celery Salad (top) and Raspberry Chicken Salad.

FAST CHICKEN

THAI CHICKEN

Preparation time: 20 minutes
Total cooking time: 20 minutes
Serves 4

8 (880 g) chicken thigh fillets
2 tablespoons oil
2 large onions, cut into eighths
2 teaspoons grated fresh
 ginger
2 cloves garlic, crushed
1 tablespoon Thai green
 curry paste
1 stem lemongrass, finely
 chopped
1 tablespoon fish sauce
 (nam pla)
3 cups coconut cream
4 medium carrots, cut into
 3 cm straws
125 g green beans, cut into
 3 cm pieces
2 tablespoons finely chopped
 fresh coriander
2 tablespoons finely chopped
 fresh mint
salt, to taste
1 cup (40 g) toasted, flaked
 coconut

➤ TRIM CHICKEN of excess fat and sinew. Cut into thin strips.
1 Heat oil in a heavy-based frying pan; add chicken. Cook over high heat for 2 minutes or until chicken is lightly browned. Remove from pan and drain on paper towels.
2 Add onion, ginger, garlic and curry paste to pan; stir over medium heat for 1 minute. Return chicken to pan. Add lemongrass, fish sauce, coconut cream, carrots and beans; bring to boil. Reduce heat; simmer, uncovered, for 10 minutes or until chicken and vegetables are tender, stirring occasionally.
3 Stir in coriander, mint and salt; sprinkle coconut over. Serve immediately with noodles or rice.

COOK'S FILE

Storage time: This recipe can be made a day ahead. Store, covered with plastic wrap, in the refrigerator.
Hints: To toast coconut, spread onto a baking tray, bake in a moderate 180°C oven 5 minutes or until golden. Use only the softer stems of lemongrass. To help release the aromatic flavour, make deep cuts in the stem, while leaving it intact, or crush with a rolling pin. Fresh lemongrass is available from Asian food suppliers, some supermarkets and larger greengrocers.
Variation: For a festive look, pile noodles or rice into a serving bowl; garnish with thinly sliced cucumber, shredded mint, grated carrot, coriander and tiny red chillies.

CAMEMBERT CHICKEN WITH CRANBERRY SAUCE

Preparation time: 10 minutes
Total cooking time: 15 minutes
Serves 4

4 (460 g) chicken breast fillets
125 g camembert cheese
2 cloves garlic, crushed
2 tablespoons finely chopped
    fresh chives
plain flour
2 tablespoons oil
1 cup white wine
2 tablespoons cranberry jelly
salt and freshly ground black
    pepper, to taste

➤ TRIM CHICKEN of excess fat and sinew.

1 Using a small, sharp knife, cut a deep pocket in each fillet. Place camembert in a small bowl and mash roughly with a fork. Add garlic and chives and mash until combined. Spoon mixture into pockets in fillets. Secure openings with toothpicks. Toss chicken lightly in flour; shake off excess.

2 Heat oil in a heavy-based frying pan. Add chicken; cook over high heat for 1 minute on each side. Reduce heat, cook for 3 minutes on each side or until chicken is cooked through. Remove from pan. Cover chicken loosely with aluminium foil while preparing sauce.

3 Add wine and cranberry jelly to pan, stirring to incorporate pan juices. Season to taste. Cook over high heat until reduced by half. Pour sauce over chicken and serve immediately.

COOK'S FILE

Storage time: Cook this dish just before serving.

1

2

3

CHICKEN AND VEGETABLE CURRY

Preparation time: 5 minutes
Total cooking time: 10 minutes
Serves 4

2 (220 g) chicken breast fillets
2 tablespoons oil
1/4 cup mild curry paste
4 cups frozen Chinese
   vegetables
2/3 cup water

1/3 cup yoghurt, lightly beaten
salt, to taste

➤ TRIM CHICKEN of excess fat and sinew.

1 Cut into 2 cm cubes. Heat oil in a heavy-based frying pan.

2 Add chicken; cook over high heat for 4 minutes or until browned, stirring occasionally. Add curry paste and vegetables to pan; mix well.

3 Add water. Bring to boil; reduce heat to a simmer and cook, covered, for 3 minutes or until vegetables and chicken are tender. Remove from heat, stir in yoghurt. Add salt and serve immediately with rice.

COOK'S FILE

Storage time: Cook this dish just before serving.

Variation: Use fresh vegetables, chopped into even-sized pieces, instead of frozen vegetables.

Hint: Curry paste is a mixture of shallots, garlic, ginger and spices with chillies and pepper. From supermarkets and Asian food stores.

LEMON AND ROSEMARY CHICKEN

Preparation time: 10 minutes
Total cooking time: 20 minutes
Serves 4

8 (920 g) large chicken
   drumsticks
60 g butter
2 cloves garlic, crushed
2 teaspoons finely grated
   lemon rind
2 tablespoons chopped fresh
   rosemary
1 tablespoon plain flour

1¹/2 cups chicken stock (see
   page 11)
2 tablespoons lemon juice
salt and freshly ground black
   pepper, to taste

➤ WIPE OVER DRUMSTICKS and
pat dry with paper towels.
1 Using a sharp knife, make two
deep cuts in the thickest section of
each drumstick.
2 Melt butter in a large, heavy-
based pan, add drumsticks. Cook
over medium heat for 2 minutes on
each side or until brown. Add garlic,
lemon rind and rosemary.
3 Blend flour with stock and lemon

juice in a small bowl or jug until
smooth. Add to pan and bring to
boil. Reduce heat and simmer, covered, for 15 minutes or until drumsticks are tender, stirring occasionally. Season and serve immediately.

COOK'S FILE

Storage time: This recipe can be
cooked up to a day ahead. Store, covered, in refrigerator. Reheat gently
just before serving.
Hint: To check whether chicken is
cooked, insert a skewer into the
thickest part of the chicken. If juice
runs clear the chicken is cooked. If it
is still pink, cook a little longer.

1

2

3

CHILLI CHICKEN WINGS

Preparation time: 10 minutes
Total cooking time: 10 minutes
Serves 4

1 medium red capsicum
1 medium green capsicum
12 (1.2 kg) chicken wings
1 egg white, lightly beaten
1/2 cup cornflour
1 tablespoon soy sauce
2 tablespoons water
2 tablespoons oil
2 cloves garlic, crushed
2 teaspoons sambal oelek
2 tablespoons black bean
    sauce
2 cups light chicken stock
    (see page 11)
salt, to taste
1/2 cup roasted unsalted
    cashews, chopped

➤ CUT CAPSICUM into thin strips.
1 Cut the chicken wings into three sections, discarding tips.
2 Combine egg white, cornflour, soy sauce and water in a medium bowl; add chicken and stir until combined.
3 Heat oil in a wok or large, heavy-based frying pan, swirling gently to coat base and sides. Add chicken wings and stir-fry over medium heat 3–4 minutes or until brown and cooked through. Remove from pan and drain on paper towels.
4 Add capsicum, garlic and sambal oelek to pan; stir-fry for 2 minutes or until capsicum is tender. Add black bean sauce, stock, salt and chicken. Bring to boil; cover and cook 2 minutes or until chicken has heated through. Sprinkle cashews over and serve immediately. Serve with steamed rice.

C O O K ' S   F I L E

Storage time: Cook this dish just before serving.
Variation: Chopped boneless chicken breast or thigh can be used instead of wings in this recipe. Serve with fresh noodles instead of rice if liked. Fresh Hokkien noodles are available from Asian food stores.
Note: Sambal oelek is Indonesian crushed hot chillies in vinegar. It is available from supermarkets and Asian food stores.

1

2

3

4

CHICKEN WITH MUSHROOMS

Preparation time: 10 minutes
Total cooking time: 20 minutes
Serves 4

4 (460 g) chicken breast fillets
30 g butter
2 tablespoons oil
4 small zucchini, sliced thinly
2 leeks, sliced thinly
2 cloves garlic, crushed
2 small fresh red chillies,
    finely chopped
150 g oyster mushrooms

1 tablespoon lime juice
1/4 cup cream
salt and freshly ground black
    pepper, to taste

➤ TRIM CHICKEN of excess fat and sinew.
1 Heat butter and oil in a heavy-based frying pan; add chicken and cook over medium heat for 4 minutes on each side or until tender. Remove from pan; drain on paper towels and keep warm.
2 Add zucchini, leeks, garlic and chopped chillies to pan. Cook over high heat for 2 minutes. Add mushrooms; cook a further 3 minutes or

until the vegetables are tender.
3 Stir in lime juice and cream and cook a further 2 minutes until heated through. Season to taste. Serve immediately with roasted capsicum and warm crusty rolls or baps.

COOK'S FILE

Storage time: Cook this dish just before serving.
Variation: If oyster mushrooms are unavailable, use button or cap mushrooms, sliced.
Hint: Wear rubber gloves when chopping hot chillies; rinse them after chopping. Avoid touching your face, as the chilli juice can burn eyes.

PAPRIKA CHICKEN DRUMSTICKS

Preparation time: 10 minutes
Total cooking time: 20 minutes
Serves 4

8 (860 g) chicken drumsticks
1 tablespoon ground sweet
    paprika
1 tablespoon oil
30 g butter
2 large onions, sliced
90 g soft cream cheese
2/3 cup tomato purée
20 g sachet instant chicken
    soup mix
2 spring onions, finely
    chopped

2 cups water
salt and freshly ground black
    pepper, to taste

➤ WIPE DRUMSTICKS and pat dry with paper towels.
1 Sprinkle drumsticks evenly with paprika.
2 Heat oil and butter in heavy-based frying pan; add chicken. Cook over medium-high heat 4 minutes or until chicken is browned, turning occasionally. Remove from pan, drain on paper towels. Keep warm.
3 Add onions, cream cheese, tomato purée, soup mix, spring onions and water and bring to boil. Reduce heat. Return chicken to pan. Simmer, covered, for 15 minutes or until chicken is tender, stirring occasionally.

Season to taste and serve immediately with fettuccini sprinkled with poppyseeds, if liked.

COOK'S FILE

Storage time: This dish can be cooked up to two days ahead. Store, covered, in refrigerator. Reheat just before serving.
Variations: Omit soup mix and substitute 2 cups of chicken stock for the 2 cups water, if liked. Or, replace 1 cup water or stock with wine.
Hint: After cooking any chicken dish ahead of time, cool it rapidly by immersing the base of the dish in iced water. Store, covered, in the refrigerator. Harmful bacteria can develop if the dish is left to cool slowly at room temperature.

*Chicken with Mushrooms (top) and
Paprika Chicken Drumsticks.*

ALMOND CHICKEN WITH BRANDY SAUCE

Preparation time: 10 minutes
Total cooking time: 15 minutes
Serves 4

4 (460 g) chicken breast fillets
1 cup (80 g) flaked almonds
2 tablespoons oil
60 g butter
2 leeks (white part only), sliced
⅓ cup brandy or cognac
⅔ cup cream
salt and freshly ground black pepper, to taste

➤ TRIM CHICKEN of excess fat and sinew.

1 Place flaked almonds in heavy-based frying pan. Stir over medium heat for 3 minutes or until golden. Remove from pan, set aside.

2 Heat oil in pan; add chicken. Cook over high heat for 1 minute on each side. Reduce heat; cook for a further 3 minutes on each side or until cooked through. Remove from pan and cover with aluminium foil. Drain oil from pan.

3 Add butter and leeks to pan. Cook over medium heat for 3 minutes or until leeks are tender. Add cognac or brandy to the pan and cook until reduced by half, stirring occasionally. Add cream, cook for 3 minutes or until sauce has thickened slightly. To serve, place chicken on individual serving plates, pour the sauce over chicken and sprinkle with flaked almonds. Serve hot with steamed seasonal vegetables.

COOK'S FILE

Storage time: Cook this dish just before serving.

CHINESE CHICKEN AND NOODLES

Preparation time: 10 minutes
Total cooking time: 15 minutes
Serves 4

6 (660 g) chicken thigh fillets
1/3 cup satay sauce
2 tablespoons soy sauce
2 tablespoons sherry
2 tablespoons oil
1 onion, cut into eighths
2 medium carrots, thinly
  sliced
125 g snow peas
4 cups (400 g) chopped bok
  choy or Chinese cabbage
2 cups bean sprouts
2 tablespoons cornflour

1 cup light chicken stock (see
  page 11)
salt, to taste
100 g fresh Chinese egg noodles

➤ TRIM CHICKEN of excess fat and sinew.
1 Cut chicken into 2 cm cubes. Combine with satay sauce, soy sauce and sherry in a large mixing bowl.
2 Heat oil in a heavy-based frying pan. Add onion and carrot and cook over high heat for 2 minutes, stirring occasionally. Add snow peas and bok choy and cook, stirring, over high heat for 1 minute. Remove from pan; set aside.
3 Add chicken mixture to pan. Cook, stirring occasionally, over high heat for 4 minutes or until chicken is tender and cooked through.

4 Return vegetables to pan. Add bean sprouts and blended cornflour and stock. Add salt, stir 2 minutes or until sauce boils and thickens. Cook noodles in a medium pan of rapidly boiling water until just tender, about 2 minutes. Drain. Place noodles in individual deep serving plates, spoon chicken and vegetables over. Serve immediately.

COOK'S FILE

Storage time: Cook this dish just before serving.

STIR-FRIED CHICKEN AND VEGETABLES

Preparation time: 15 minutes
Total cooking time: 10 minutes
Serves 4

4 (460 g) chicken breast fillets
1/4 cup oil
1 medium green capsicum, sliced
200 g sugar snap peas or snow peas
8 cups (750 g) sliced Chinese cabbage

4 spring onions, cut into 3 cm pieces
2 cloves garlic, crushed
2 teaspoons grated ginger
1 tablespoon cornflour
1 cup light chicken stock (see page 11)
1 tablespoon oyster sauce
1 tablespoon sherry
salt, to taste

➤ TRIM CHICKEN of excess fat and sinew. Cut into thin strips.

1 Heat oil in heavy-based frying pan or wok, swirling gently to coat base and sides. Add chicken and stir-fry over high heat 4 minutes or until browned. Remove from pan; drain on paper towels. Keep warm.

2 Add capsicum and peas; stir-fry for 2 minutes. Add cabbage, spring onions, garlic and ginger; stir-fry for 1 minute. Return chicken to pan.

3 Blend cornflour with stock, oyster sauce and sherry until smooth. Add to ingredients in pan. Stir over medium heat for 1 minute or until sauce boils and thickens and chicken and vegetables are tender. Add salt to taste, serve immediately.

COOK'S FILE

Storage time: Cook this dish just before serving.

CRISPY SPICED CHICKEN WINGS

Preparation time: 5 minutes
Total cooking time: 6 minutes
Serves 4–6

12 (1.2 kg) chicken wings
2 teaspoons ground cumin
2 teaspoons ground coriander
2 teaspoons ground cardamom
2 teaspoons ground turmeric
2 teaspoons ground chilli

salt, to taste
oil for deep frying
1/3 cup fruit chutney

➤ WIPE CHICKEN wings.

1 Pat wings completely dry with paper towels.

2 Combine cumin, coriander, cardamom, turmeric, chilli and salt in a large bowl. Add chicken wings, toss to coat completely. Use fingers to rub spices well into the chicken.

3 Heat oil in a deep heavy-based pan until moderately hot. Cook chicken, in two batches, for 3 minutes each batch or until golden brown and cooked through. Drain on paper towels. Arrange on a serving platter and serve hot with chutney as an appetiser.

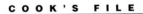

COOK'S FILE

Storage time: Cook just before serving. Chicken can be coated with spices several hours ahead. Store, covered, in the refrigerator.

Variation: Plum and peanut or satay sauces are also delicious served with this dish.

1

2

3

CHICKEN BREASTS WITH CURRIED MANGO SAUCE

Preparation time: 10 minutes
Total cooking time: 15 minutes
Serves 4

4 (460 g) chicken breast fillets
1 tablespoon oil
30 g butter
4 spring onions, chopped
2 cloves garlic, crushed

1 tablespoon curry powder
170 g can mango pulp
1/3 cup sour cream
1 tablespoon seeded mustard
1/2 cup light chicken stock
salt and freshly ground black
    pepper, to taste

➤ TRIM CHICKEN of excess fat and sinew.

1 Heat oil and butter in pan; add chicken fillets. Cook over medium heat for 4 minutes on each side or until lightly browned and cooked through. Remove from pan, cover with aluminium foil. Keep warm.

2 Add spring onions, garlic and curry powder to pan juices; stir over medium heat for 1 minute.

3 Add mango, sour cream, mustard and stock to pan. Bring to boil, reduce heat; simmer 3 minutes until heated through, stirring occasionally. Season, pour over chicken and serve.

COOK'S FILE

Storage time: Cook this dish just before serving.

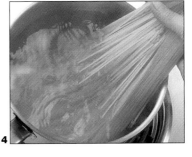

SPAGHETTI WITH CHICKEN BOLOGNAISE

Preparation time: 10 minutes
Total cooking time: 15 minutes
Serves 4

2 leeks
1 red capsicum
2 tablespoons olive oil
2 cloves garlic, crushed
500 g chicken mince
2 cups tomato pasta sauce
1 tablespoon chopped
    fresh thyme
1 tablespoon chopped
    fresh rosemary
2 tablespoons seeded and
    chopped black olives
salt and freshly ground black
    pepper, to taste
400 g spaghetti
125 g feta cheese,
    crumbled

➤ WASH LEEKS WELL. Cut into thin slices (white part only).

1 Finely chop capsicum. Heat oil in large, heavy-based pan; add leek, capsicum and garlic and cook over medium-high heat for 2 minutes or until lightly browned.

2 Add chicken mince; cook over high heat for 3 minutes or until browned and any liquid has evaporated. Stir occasionally and break up any lumps as mince cooks.

3 Add tomato pasta sauce, thyme and rosemary and bring to boil. Reduce heat and simmer, uncovered, for 5 minutes or until sauce has reduced and thickened. Add olives, stir to combine. Season to taste.

4 Cook spaghetti in a large pan of rapidly boiling water with a little oil added until just tender; drain. Place spaghetti on individual serving plates or pile into a large deep serving dish and pour Chicken Bolognaise over. (Sauce can be mixed through pasta.) Sprinkle with feta and serve immediately.

COOK'S FILE

Storage time: Chicken Bolognaise can be cooked up to two days ahead. Store, covered, in the refrigerator, or freeze for up to four weeks. Reheat sauce and cook spaghetti just before serving.

Variation: Any type of pasta, dried or fresh, is suitable to use. Freshly grated parmesan or pecorino can be used instead of feta cheese.

FETTUCCINE WITH CHICKEN AND MUSHROOM SAUCE

Preparation time: 10 minutes
Total cooking time: 20 minutes
Serves 4

2 (330 g) chicken breast fillets
1 tablespoon olive oil
30 g butter
2 rashers bacon, trimmed and
    cut into thin strips
2 cloves garlic, crushed
250 g button mushrooms,
    sliced
1/3 cup white wine
2/3 cup cream
4 spring onions, chopped
1 tablespoon plain flour
2 tablespoons water
salt and freshly ground black
    pepper, to taste
400 g fettuccine
1/3 cup grated parmesan cheese

➤ TRIM CHICKEN of excess fat and sinew.

1 Cut chicken into thin strips. Heat oil and butter in a heavy-based frying pan; add chicken and cook over medium heat for 3 minutes or until browned.

2 Add bacon, garlic and mushrooms; cook over medium heat for 2 minutes, stirring occasionally.

3 Add wine and cook until liquid has reduced by half. Add cream and spring onions and bring to boil. Blend flour with water until smooth. Add to pan and stir over heat until the mixture boils and thickens; reduce heat and simmer for 2 minutes. Season to taste.

4 Cook fettuccine in large pan of rapidly boiling water with a little oil added. Drain. Add fettuccine to sauce and stir over low heat until combined. Sprinkle with parmesan. Serve immediately with a green salad and hot herb bread (see Note).

COOK'S FILE

Storage time: The sauce for this dish can be made one day ahead. Reheat sauce and cook pasta just before serving.

Variation: Any type of dried or fresh pasta can be used.

Hint: Scrub cutting boards thoroughly in hot soapy water to remove all traces of chicken. Make sure wooden boards have a smooth surface. A rough, cracked surface can harbour harmful bacteria.

Note: To make herb bread, combine 120 g butter (softened) with 1/2 cup chopped mixed fresh herbs and a finely chopped garlic clove. Slice a medium breadstick diagonally; spread each piece with herb butter. Reshape into a loaf, wrap in aluminium foil and bake in a moderate 180°C oven for 30 minutes or until loaf is crisp and hot.

1

2

3

4

Fettuccine with Chicken and Mushroom Sauce.

CHICKEN DIANE

Preparation time: 10 minutes
Total cooking time: 15 minutes
Serves 4

8 (880 g) chicken thigh
    fillets
2 tablespoons parsley
90 g butter
2 cloves garlic, crushed

1 tablespoon Worcestershire
    sauce
1/3 cup sour cream
2 tablespoons cream
salt and freshly ground black
    pepper, to taste

➤ TRIM CHICKEN of excess fat and
sinew.
1 Finely chop parsley. Melt butter in
a heavy-based frying pan. Add garlic.
2 Add chicken, cook on medium

heat for 4 minutes on each side or
until cooked through. Remove from
pan and set aside. Keep warm.
3 Add Worcestershire sauce, parsley and both creams. Stir over medium heat for 1 minute. Season to
taste. Return chicken to pan, coat
with sauce and serve.

COOK'S FILE

Storage time: Cook this dish just
before serving.

1

2

3

CHICKEN WITH GINGER PLUM SAUCE

Preparation time: 15 minutes
Total cooking time: 10 minutes
Serves 4

4 (460 g) chicken breast fillets
2 tablespoons cornflour
1/2 teaspoon Chinese five-spice
   powder
850 g can plums, drained,
   seeded
1 cup water
1 tablespoon oil
1 tablespoon sesame oil
2 medium onions, cut into
   eighths
2 stalks celery, sliced
   diagonally
1 small cucumber, halved
   lengthways, sliced
2 cloves garlic, crushed
2 teaspoons grated fresh ginger
1 tablespoon soy sauce
425 g can lychees, drained
salt, to taste

➤ TRIM CHICKEN of excess fat and sinew. Cut into 2 cm cubes.

1 Combine cornflour and five-spice powder in a bowl; add chicken cubes and toss until coated.

2 Place plums and water in blender or food processor bowl. Using the pulse action, process for 10 seconds or until smooth.

3 Heat oil in a wok or large, heavy-based pan, swirling gently to coat base and sides. Add the chicken and stir-fry over high heat for 2 minutes until brown. Remove and drain on paper towels. Add sesame oil, onion and celery to pan; stir-fry for 2 minutes or until tender. Add cucumber, garlic and ginger; stir-fry 1 minute.

4 Return chicken to pan with plum purée, soy sauce and lychees; stir gently until sauce has boiled and thickened. Season and serve immediately with steamed rice.

COOK'S FILE

Storage time: Cook this dish just before serving.
Note: Chinese five-spice powder is a blend of Chinese brown peppercorns, cinnamon bark, cloves, fennel and star anise.
Hint: Store all spices in an airtight container in a cool dry place.

1

2

3

4

SESAME CHICKEN WITH TAHINI CREAM

Preparation time: 15 minutes
Total cooking time: 20 minutes
Serves 4

4 (460 g) chicken breast
   fillets
2 tablespoons olive oil
1/2 cup packaged breadcrumbs
1/4 cup sesame seeds
2 tablespoons ground
   cumin
1 teaspoon ground chilli
salt and freshly ground black
   pepper, to taste

Tahini Cream
1/3 cup tahini
1/3 cup sour cream
1 tablespoon lemon juice
1 tablespoon finely chopped
   fresh coriander leaves
2 spring onions, finely chopped

➤ PREHEAT OVEN to moderately hot 210°C/190°C gas. Trim chicken of excess fat and sinew. Brush chicken fillets with oil.
1 Combine the breadcrumbs with sesame seeds, cumin, chilli, salt and pepper. Coat chicken with mixture.
2 Place chicken in a shallow baking tray. Bake 20 minutes or until cooked through and lightly golden.

3 To make Tahini Cream: Place tahini, sour cream, lemon juice, coriander and spring onions in a small bowl; stir until combined. Serve with hot Sesame Chicken. Serve dish with pitta or Lebanese bread.

COOK'S FILE

Storage time: Cook chicken just before serving. Tahini Cream can be made one day ahead. Store, covered, in the refrigerator. Bring to room temperature to serve.
Hint: Tahini is a nutritious paste made from ground sesame seeds. It is used in Middle Eastern dishes. It is available from supermarkets, health food stores and delicatessens.

CHICKEN DRUMSTICKS WITH PESTO SAUCE

Preparation time: 10 minutes
Total cooking time: 15 minutes
Serves 4

1/3 cup pine nuts
1 cup firmly packed fresh
   basil leaves
1 cup firmly packed fresh
   parsley
2 cloves garlic, crushed
1/2 cup grated parmesan
   cheese
2/3 cup crème fraîche
1 cup water

2 tablespoons oil
8 (856 g) chicken drumsticks
salt and freshly ground black
   pepper to taste

➤ PLACE PINE NUTS on an oven tray. Cook under grill, medium-high heat, 2–3 minutes or until golden. Watch carefully as the pine nuts will colour quickly.
1 Place pine nuts, basil, parsley, garlic, cheese, crème fraîche and water in food processor bowl or blender. Using the pulse action, press button 10 seconds or until mixture is smooth. Pour into a bowl; cover with plastic wrap.
2 Heat oil in a heavy-based frying

pan; add chicken. Cook over medium heat for 10 minutes or until cooked through and browned, turning occasionally. Drain on paper towels; keep warm. Wipe pan with paper towels.
3 Add sauce to pan; stir over medium heat until boiling. Season to taste and pour over chicken to serve.

COOK'S FILE

Storage time: Sauce can be made up to one hour ahead. Cover surface of sauce completely with plastic wrap to prevent discolouration. Cook chicken just before serving.
Note: Crème fraîche is a very soft white cream cheese, similar in flavour to sour cream.

Sesame Chicken with Tahini Cream (top)
and Chicken Drumsticks with Pesto Sauce.

SPECIAL OCCASION

CHICKEN TEMPURA WITH SEAFOOD

Preparation time: 25 minutes,
  + 2 hours refrigeration
  + 1 hour standing
Total cooking time: 10 minutes
Serves 4

3 (345 g) chicken breast fillets
1 tablespoon soy sauce
2 teaspoons sugar
1 tablespoon lemon juice
1 cup cornflour
1 egg, separated
¼ cup water
200 g scallops
200 g green, medium prawns
20 g butter
2 teaspoons cornflour, extra
2 tablespoons lemon juice
1 chicken stock cube, crumbled
¼ teaspoon dried oregano
1 tablespoon white wine
salt and freshly ground black
    pepper, to taste
1 small red chilli, finely
    shredded
2 tablespoons butter, chopped,
    extra
¼ cup oil

➤ TRIM CHICKEN fillets of excess fat and sinew.

1 Cut each chicken fillet into four long strips; place in a medium mixing bowl. Add combined soy, sugar and juice; mix well. Cover with plastic wrap, refrigerate 2 hours.
Combine cornflour, egg yolk and water in a small mixing bowl; beat until smooth. Cover with plastic wrap and set aside for 1 hour.

2 Rinse and drain scallops. Peel prawns, leaving tails intact; devein. Heat butter in a medium heavy-based pan; add seafood. Stir over high heat for 1 minute; remove from pan and keep warm. Add extra cornflour, lemon juice, stock cube, oregano and wine to pan. Stir over low heat 3 minutes or until mixture is smooth. Season to taste; add chilli. Stir until mixture boils and thickens. Remove from heat; add seafood and extra butter. Stir until butter melts. Keep warm.

3 Place egg white in small, dry mixing bowl. Using a whisk, beat until soft peaks form. Using a metal spoon, fold into cornflour mixture. Heat oil in shallow frying pan. Dip chicken, a few pieces at a time, into batter; add to pan. Cook in batches over medium heat 2 minutes each side until just golden and tender. Drain on paper towels. Serve immediately with seafood and vegetables.

COOK'S FILE

Storage time: Cook this dish just before serving.

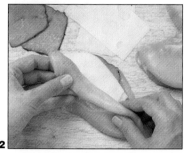

CHICKEN CORDON BLEU

Preparation time: 15 minutes,
  + 30 minutes refrigeration
Total cooking time: 16 minutes
Serves 4

4 (460 g) chicken breast fillets
salt and freshly ground black
  pepper, to taste
4 thick slices Swiss cheese
4 slices double-smoked ham or
  pastrami

1/3 cup seasoned flour
1 egg, lightly beaten
1/2 cup packaged breadcrumbs
1/2 cup oil

➤ TRIM CHICKEN of excess fat and
sinew. Remove skin.
1 Using a sharp knife, cut into thickest section of each fillet without cutting right through. Open fillet out
flat. Season to taste.
2 Place a slice of cheese and ham on
one side of each fillet. Fold remaining
half of fillet over to enclose filling.

3 Carefully coat each fillet with
flour; shake off excess. Dip into egg,
then coat with breadcrumbs. Place on
a foil-lined tray. Place, covered, in
refrigerator for 30 minutes.
4 Heat oil in medium heavy-based
pan; add chicken. Cook over medium
heat for 4 minutes each side or until
chicken is golden and cooked
through. Serve immediately.

COOK'S FILE

Storage time: This dish is best
made just before serving.

SPICY STUFFED CHICKEN WINGS

Preparation time: 40 minutes
Total cooking time: 25 minutes
Serves 4

8 (800 g) large chicken wings
1/2 cup finely chopped water
   chestnuts
2 small onions, grated
6 spring onions, finely chopped
2 medium tomatoes, seeded,
   finely chopped
2 medium cucumbers, finely
   chopped
1/2 cup finely chopped fresh
   coriander leaves
1 tablespoon sweet chilli sauce
salt, to taste
2 slices wholemeal bread,
   finely chopped
2 tablespoons oil
3 chillies, finely chopped
1 clove garlic, crushed
2 teaspoons curry powder
1 teaspoon ground cumin
1 teaspoon sugar
2 tablespoons lime juice

➤ PREHEAT OVEN to moderate 180°C. Wipe chicken and pat dry with paper towels.

1 Using a small sharp knife and starting at the drumstick end, slip knife down sides of bone towards the joint, without piercing the skin.

2 Snap the bone free. Proceed with the next joint in the same way, taking care not to pierce the elbow. Remove the bones; reshape the wing.

3 Combine water chestnuts, onions, tomatoes, cucumbers, coriander, chilli sauce, salt and bread in a medium mixing bowl; mix well. Divide the mixture into eight portions. Use a spoon to stuff each wing with the filling. Secure end with a toothpick.

4 Heat the oil in large heavy-based pan; add chillies, garlic, curry powder and cumin. Stir over medium heat for 30 seconds. Add chicken and turn gently to coat with flavourings. Cook over medium heat 2 minutes each side or until golden but not cooked through. Transfer chicken to a shallow ovenproof dish. Add sugar and lime juice to pan juices. Stir and bring to boil. Pour mixture over wings. Bake 20 minutes or until just tender. Serve hot, with pan juices as a sauce. Serve with noodles or rice.

COOK'S FILE

Storage time: This dish is best made just before serving.

CHICKEN MARSALA

Preparation time: 5 minutes
Total cooking time: 18 minutes
Serves 4

4 (460 g) chicken breast fillets
2 tablespoons oil
60 g butter
1 clove garlic, crushed
2 cups chicken stock (see
    page 11)
1/3 cup marsala
2 teaspoons plain flour
1/4 cup cream
2 teaspoons Worcestershire
    sauce

salt and freshly ground black
    pepper, to taste

➤ TRIM CHICKEN of excess fat and sinew.

1 Heat oil in a heavy-based frying pan; add chicken. Cook over medium heat for 4 minutes on each side or until cooked through and lightly golden. Remove chicken, cover with aluminium foil and keep warm. Drain off any fat from pan.

2 Add butter and garlic to the pan; stir over medium heat for 2 minutes. Add stock and marsala; bring to boil. Reduce heat and simmer 5 minutes or until the liquid has reduced by half.

3 Stir in the blended flour, cream and Worcestershire sauce; stir over medium heat until sauce boils and thickens. Season to taste. Pour over chicken. Serve hot, with purple or green brussels sprouts and pasta.

COOK'S FILE

Storage time: Cook this dish just before serving.

Variations: Marsala is a sweet wine and makes a sweet-tasting sauce. Port or dry red wine can be substituted. Chicken thighs or drumsticks can be used instead of breast fillets.

Hint: Boiling wine or spirits during cooking evaporates the alcohol, leaving the flavour without any intoxicating effects.

1

2

3

BAKED CHICKEN ROLLS

Preparation time: 35 minutes
Total cooking time: 20 minutes
Serves 4

8 (750 g) chicken thigh fillets
125 g sun-dried tomatoes
1/2 cup grated cheddar cheese
1/3 cup firmly packed fresh
     basil leaves
8 slices prosciutto or leg ham

Warm Mustard Dressing
1/3 cup olive oil
1 tablespoon balsamic vinegar
2 cloves garlic, crushed
2 teaspoons mustard
salt, to taste

➤ PREHEAT OVEN to moderate 180°C. Remove excess fat and sinew from chicken.

1 Lay thigh fillets out, smooth-side down, on work surface. Place a sheet of plastic wrap over chicken and flatten lightly using a meat mallet or rolling pin.

2 Place sun-dried tomatoes, cheese and basil in food processor bowl or blender. Using the pulse action, process for 10 seconds or until mixture is finely chopped.

3 Spoon mixture onto end of each thigh fillet. Roll fillets to enclose mixture. Wrap each roll firmly in a slice of prosciutto. Place rolls into a shallow baking dish. Bake for 20 minutes or until cooked through. Serve immediately with Warm Mustard Dressing. Serve with fresh pasta and grilled eggplant or salad.

4 To make Warm Mustard Dressing: Combine all ingredients in a small pan; stir over medium heat until hot.

COOK'S FILE

Storage time: Rolls can be assembled up to two hours ahead and refrigerated. Cook just before serving.
Hint: Prosciutto is also known as Parma ham. It is available, thinly sliced, from delicatessens.

PESTO CHICKEN WITH FRESH TOMATO SAUCE

Preparation time: 30 minutes
Total cooking time: 30 minutes
Serves 4

4 (460 g) chicken breast fillets
1/2 cup firmly packed fresh basil leaves
1/4 cup firmly packed fresh parsley
1 clove garlic, crushed
1 teaspoon finely grated lemon rind
1/2 cup slivered almonds, roasted
2 tablespoons olive oil
2 tablespoons olive oil, extra

Fresh Tomato Sauce
2 tablespoons olive oil
1 medium onion, chopped
4 medium tomatoes, peeled
1 tablespoon tomato paste
1 teaspoon sugar
1/3 cup water
185 g can pimiento, drained, chopped
salt and freshly ground black pepper, to taste

➤ PREHEAT OVEN to moderate 180°C. Trim chicken of excess fat and sinew.

1 Lay chicken fillets cut-side up on work surface. Cover chicken with plastic wrap and flatten lightly, by hitting with a meat mallet or rolling pin.

2 Place basil, parsley, garlic, rind and almonds in food processor or blender. Add oil slowly in a thin steady stream, blending until all oil is added and mixture is finely chopped.

3 Divide pesto mixture between chicken fillets; spread evenly. Fold fillets in half to enclose mixture. Secure with toothpicks or skewers.

4 Heat extra oil in a shallow baking dish on stovetop; add chicken. Cook for 2 minutes on each side or until

lightly browned. Transfer baking dish to the oven; cook, uncovered, for 15 minutes or until chicken is tender and cooked through.

5 To make Fresh Tomato Sauce: Heat oil in pan; add onion; cook over medium heat 5 minutes or until just tender; do not brown.

Remove seeds from tomato and discard. Chop flesh roughly. Add tomato, tomato paste, sugar and water to pan; bring to boil. Reduce heat and cook, covered, 5 minutes or until tomato is soft but still holding its shape.

6 Add pimiento; cook until heated through, season to taste. Pour over chicken. Serve immediately with artichoke hearts or other seasonal vegetables, salad and bread rolls.

C O O K ' S   F I L E

Storage time: Chicken fillets can be prepared up to two hours ahead; cook just before serving.

Fresh Tomato Sauce can be prepared up to two days ahead. Store, covered, in refrigerator; reheat gently just before serving.

Hint: To roast almonds, spread over a shallow oven tray; bake in moderate 180°C oven for 10 minutes or until lightly browned. Leave to cool.

BLUE CHEESE CHICKEN WITH APPLE CHUTNEY SAUCE

Preparation time: 20 minutes
Total cooking time: 25 minutes
Serves 4

4 (460 g) chicken breast fillets
60 g blue vein cheese
60 g ricotta cheese
2 teaspoons French mustard
1/4 cup chopped walnuts
60 g butter, melted

Apple Chutney Sauce
2 tablespoons oil
1 leek (white part only), finely
    sliced
2 cloves garlic, crushed
2 red apples, peeled, quartered,
    cored and sliced
1/3 cup fruit chutney
2 tablespoons finely chopped
    fresh chives
salt and freshly ground black
    pepper, to taste

➤ PREHEAT OVEN to moderate 180°C. Trim chicken of excess fat and sinew.

1 Using a small, sharp knife, cut a deep pocket in each breast fillet.

2 Combine blue vein and ricotta cheeses with mustard and walnuts in a medium bowl; mix well. Spoon mixture into pockets in chicken. Secure openings with toothpicks.

3 Place chicken in a shallow baking dish and brush with butter. Bake for 20 minutes or until cooked through and lightly browned, turning occasionally. Remove toothpicks. Place chicken on a warmed serving platter and pour Apple Chutney Sauce around. Serve immediately.

4 To make Apple Chutney Sauce: Heat oil in a medium heavy-based pan; add leek and garlic and stir over medium heat for 2 minutes or until leek is tender. Add apple; cook 2 minutes or until apple is tender. Stir in chutney and chives, season to taste; stir until heated through.

COOK'S FILE

Storage time: Chicken can be assembled up to four hours ahead. Cook just before serving. Apple Chutney Sauce can be made one day ahead. Store, covered, in refrigerator.

ROAST BABY CHICKENS WITH PEPPERCORN CHEESE SAUCE

Preparation time: 10 minutes
Total cooking time: 55 minutes
Serves 4

2 x 400 g baby chickens
2 large onions, cut into
　eighths
2 tablespoons olive oil
freshly ground black pepper,
　to taste
1/4 cup brandy or cognac

1 cup light chicken stock (see
　page 11)
1 tablespoon chopped fresh sage
125 g soft peppercorn cheese
salt, to taste

➤ PREHEAT OVEN to moderate 180°C. Remove giblets and any large deposits of fat from the chickens. Wipe and pat dry with paper towels.
1 Using poultry shears, halve chickens lengthways. Place onions into shallow baking dish; pour over oil, mix well. Sprinkle with pepper. Place chickens, cut-side down, on onions.
2 Bake for 45 minutes or until golden and cooked through. Remove chickens from baking dish; keep warm while making sauce.
3 Place baking dish with onions on stovetop. Add brandy; cook over medium heat until reduced by half. Add stock and sage; bring to boil. Add cheese, reduce heat and stir until cheese has melted and mixture is combined. Season to taste. Place chickens on individual serving plates, pour sauce over and serve.

COOK'S FILE

Storage time: Cook this dish just before serving.

MEDITERRANEAN CHICKEN PARCELS

Preparation time: 20 minutes
Total cooking time: 50 minutes
Serves 4

4 (440 g) chicken thigh fillets
2 tablespoons oil
60 g black olives, pitted,
    chopped
2 cloves garlic, crushed
1 tablespoon fresh thyme
    leaves
200 g cherry tomatoes,
    halved
salt and freshly ground black
    pepper, to taste
8 sheets filo pastry
90 g melted butter

Cream Sauce
1/2 cup cream
1 tablespoon seeded mustard
2 teaspoons balsamic vinegar
2 tablespoons finely chopped
    fresh basil
125 g feta cheese, crumbled

➤ PREHEAT OVEN to moderate 180°C. Trim chicken of excess fat and sinew.

1 Heat oil in heavy-based frying pan; add chicken. Cook over medium heat 4 minutes on each side or until lightly browned and just cooked. Remove from pan; drain on paper towels.

2 Add olives, garlic, thyme and tomatoes to pan. Stir over medium heat for 1 minute or until tomatoes are tender but still holding their shape. Season, remove from heat; cool.

3 Lay a sheet of pastry on a flat work surface. Brush sheet all over with melted butter. Top with another sheet. Place a chicken fillet on one corner of the pastry sheet; top with one-quarter of the tomato mixture. Roll up, tucking in the ends as you go. Place seam-side down on a shallow baking tray. Repeat with remaining pastry, chicken and tomato mixture to make four parcels.

4 Bake, uncovered, 30 minutes or until golden. Remove from oven and place on warmed serving platter or individual plates. Pour Cream Sauce over and serve immediately.

To make Cream Sauce: Combine cream, mustard, balsamic vinegar, chopped basil and feta cheese in a medium heavy-based pan. Stir over medium heat until heated through.

COOK'S FILE

Storage time: Chicken fillets and tomato mixture can be cooked one day ahead. Store, covered, in refrigerator. Assemble parcels and cook just before serving.

Hint: To prevent filo drying out while working, cover pastry with a damp tea-towel.

1

2

3

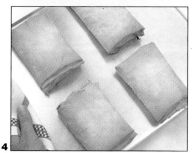
4

1

2

3

4

CHICKEN FLORENTINE WITH ROAST CAPSICUM

Preparation time: 35 minutes
Total cooking time: 45 minutes
Serves 4

4 (1.7 kg) chicken maryland
   pieces
12 English spinach leaves
250 g ricotta cheese
1/2 cup grated parmesan
   cheese
3 cloves garlic, crushed
1 medium onion, thinly
   sliced
salt and freshly ground black
   pepper, to taste
60 g butter, melted
2 large red capsicum, halved,
   seeds removed

➤ PREHEAT OVEN to moderate 180°C. Trim chicken of excess fat and sinew.

1 Gently ease the skin away from the chicken flesh, leaving skin attached along one side.

2 Remove stalks from spinach; add leaves to a medium pan of simmering water. Cover and cook for 2 minutes or until tender. Remove from heat; drain and squeeze out excess liquid. Chop spinach finely.

3 Combine spinach with ricotta, parmesan and garlic in medium bowl. Spoon mixture carefully between skin and flesh of chicken. Use toothpicks to secure opening. Place chicken in shallow baking dish. Top with onion rings, salt and black pepper to taste; drizzle with melted butter. Bake 45 minutes or until golden and cooked through.

4 Place capsicum cut-side down on a shallow baking tray. Bake 30 minutes or until skin lifts away from flesh. Peel skin off capsicum, slice and serve with chicken.

COOK'S FILE

Storage time: Chicken Florentine can be assembled a day ahead. Store, covered with plastic wrap, in the refrigerator. Cook just before serving. Roast capsicum can be cooked a day ahead and refrigerated. Reheat in oven while chicken is cooking.

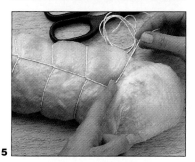

CHICKEN ROLL WITH ORANGE SAUCE

Preparation time: 1 hour
 + 10 minutes standing
Total cooking time: 1 hour 45 minutes
Serves 6

1.8 kg chicken
2 tablespoons olive oil

Filling
125 g dried apricots
250 g leg ham, chopped
1 cup fresh soft breadcrumbs
1 cup cooked brown and wild
    rice mix
1/2 cup shelled pistachio nuts
2 spring onions, chopped
2 eggs, lightly beaten
1 tablespoon canned green
    peppercorns, rinsed
    and drained
salt, to taste

Orange Sauce
2 cups light chicken stock (see
    page 11)
2 tablespoons Grand Marnier
2 tablespoons thinly shredded
    orange rind
1 tablespoon cornflour
2 tablespoons orange juice

➤ PREHEAT OVEN to moderate
180°C.
1 To bone chicken: Cut through
the skin along the centre back. Using
the tip of a small sharp knife, separate
flesh from bone down one side to the
breast, without piercing the skin.
2 Follow the bones closely with the
knife, gradually easing the meat from
the thigh, drumstick and wing. Cut
through thigh bone and cut off wing
tip as you go.
3 Repeat on other side, then lift the
ribcage away, leaving the flesh in one
piece. Turn wing and drumsticks
inside the chicken. Lay chicken out
flat, skin-side down.

4 To make Filling: Place apricots
in small bowl; cover with boiling
water. Stand 10 minutes to soften;
drain. Combine remaining filling
ingredients; press evenly over chicken.
Lay apricots in a line across the centre,
from one drumstick to the other.
5 Roll chicken to enclose filling,
tucking in ends as you go. Secure

with toothpicks. Tie chicken at intervals with string to help retain its shape. Pour the oil into shallow baking dish. Place chicken in dish; bake for 1 hour 30 minutes or until golden brown and cooked through. Remove from oven and keep warm, covered with foil.

6 To make Orange Sauce: Transfer baking dish to stovetop. Add stock to pan juices; stir over high heat until boiling. Add liqueur and rind. Reduce heat; simmer for 2 minutes. Blend cornflour with orange juice until smooth. Add to pan; stir 2 minutes or until sauce has boiled and thickened. Remove from heat. Remove string from chicken, slice and serve with Orange Sauce.

COOK'S FILE

Storage time: This dish can be assembled a day ahead. Store, covered, in refrigerator. Cook just before serving. Chicken Roll can also be served cold and will keep in the refrigerator for up to two days.

Variation: Chicken or veal mince can be substituted for leg ham.

BABY CHICKENS IN RED WINE

Preparation time: 25 minutes
Total cooking time: 1 hour 5 minutes
Serves 4

2 x 400 g baby chickens
plain flour
¼ cup olive oil
16 baby onions
125 g bacon pieces, chopped
2 cloves garlic, crushed
3 cups red wine
½ cup brandy or cognac
4 bay leaves

1 tablespoon fresh thyme
leaves
250 g button mushrooms
salt and freshly ground black
pepper, to taste

➤ REMOVE GIBLETS and any large deposits of fat from the chickens. Wipe and pat dry with paper towels.

1 Using poultry shears cut chickens into quarters. Toss lightly in flour; shake off excess.

2 Heat oil in a large heavy-based pan; add chicken. Cook for 2 minutes on each side or until lightly browned. Add onions, bacon, garlic, wine, brandy, bay leaves and thyme. Bring to boil, reduce heat and cook, covered, for 30 minutes, stirring occasionally.

3 Add mushrooms; continue cooking for 30 minutes more or until chicken is tender. Remove lid for last 15 minutes of cooking to thicken sauce. Season to taste. Serve hot.

COOK'S FILE

Storage time: This dish can be made up to two days ahead. Store, covered, in refrigerator. Reheat gently just before serving.

Hint: Any robust red wine such as burgundy or claret would be ideal for use in this recipe.

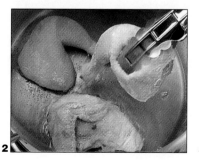

CHICKEN MOROCCO

Preparation time: 10 minutes
Total cooking time: 1 hour
Serves 4

4 (1.7 kg) chicken maryland
 pieces
2 tablespoons oil
2 small onions
2 cloves garlic
2 teaspoons grated fresh ginger
1 teaspoon ground cinnamon
1 teaspoon ground cumin
1 teaspoon ground turmeric
2 cups chicken stock (see
 page 11)
2 tablespoons finely chopped
 fresh parsley
2 tablespoons finely chopped
 fresh coriander

1/3 cup lemon juice
12 green olives, pitted, chopped
2 teaspoons grated lemon rind

➤ PREHEAT OVEN to moderate 180°C. Trim chicken of excess fat and sinew. Place chicken in single layer in a shallow ovenproof dish.
1 Chop onions finely. Crush garlic.
2 Heat oil in medium pan; add onion, garlic and ginger. Cook over medium heat for 2 minutes or until onion is tender. Add cinnamon, cumin and turmeric; cook 1 minute. Add stock; stir until combined. Remove from heat.
3 Pour mixture over chicken. Cover dish with a lid or aluminium foil. Bake 1 hour or until chicken is tender, turning occasionally. Remove from oven; transfer to serving plates. Scoop any fat from surface of sauce.

4 Stir in parsley, coriander and lemon juice. Spoon sauce over chicken. Sprinkle with olives and lemon rind. Serve with couscous or rice.

COOK'S FILE

Storage time: This dish can be cooked a day ahead. Store, covered, in refrigerator. Reheat in moderate oven for 30 minutes.
Hint: Instant couscous is available from delicatessens. Soak for 10 minutes in water or stock, then heat with a little butter. Serve hot.

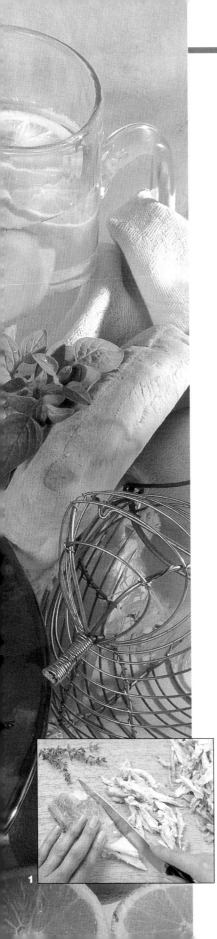

READY-TO-GO

recipes with take-away or pre-cooked chicken

CHICKEN SALAD WITH QUICK HERB SAUCE

Preparation time: 20 minutes
Total cooking time: Nil
Serves 4–6

1 barbecued chicken
1 small Lebanese cucumber
1 red capsicum
3 spring onions
1 red onion
1 green oak leaf lettuce

Quick Herb Sauce
2 egg yolks
150 g butter, melted
3 tablespoons lemon juice
1 tablespoon freshly chopped
  chives
3 teaspoons freshly chopped
  lemon thyme
1 teaspoon seeded mustard
salt and freshly ground black
  pepper, to taste

➤ REMOVE MEAT from chicken carcass; discard bones.
1 Shred meat into bite-size pieces. Cut cucumber in half lengthways. Cut each half into thin diagonal slices. Remove and discard seeds and membrane from capsicum. Cut into long, thin strips. Finely slice spring onions. Cut red onion into thin slices. Thoroughly wash and drain lettuce. Tear into small pieces. Combine chicken, cucumber, capsicum, onions and lettuce in large mixing bowl. Toss until well combined.
2 To make Quick Herb Sauce: Place egg yolks in food processor bowl. Using the pulse action, process 20 seconds or until yolk is blended. With motor constantly running, add butter slowly in a thin, steady stream, processing until all butter is added and the mixture is thick and creamy.
3 Add lemon juice, chives, thyme and mustard. Process 15 seconds or until mixture is well combined. Season to taste. To serve, arrange salad in a large serving bowl or platter, drizzle sauce over and serve immediately.

COOK'S FILE

Storage time: Chicken Salad can be assembled several hours ahead. Cover and store in refrigerator. Add Quick Herb Sauce just before serving.

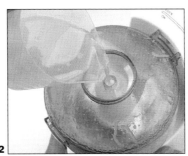

One-step recipes

CHICKEN MELTS

Remove skin and shred meat of half a BBQ chicken. Preheat grill to medium-high. Cut two 2 cm thick slices from a large loaf of brown or white bread. Spread with cream cheese. Top with chicken, sliced avocado and thinly sliced jarslberg cheese. Season to taste. Grill for 3 minutes, until cheese is golden. Serve hot.   Makes 2

CHICKEN AND CORN SOUP

Remove skin and shred meat of one BBQ chicken. Heat 3 cups chicken stock in a medium pan. Add chicken, 440 g can creamed corn, 270 g can corn kernels, 1/2 teaspoon soy sauce, mix well. Bring to the boil, reduce heat and simmer gently 4 minutes. Stir in 2 finely sliced spring onions. Season to taste.   Serves 4

CURRIED CHICKEN

Cut one BBQ chicken into 10 serving pieces and arrange on a bed of lettuce leaves in serving dish. In a bowl, combine 3/4 cup prepared mayonnaise, 2 teaspoons curry powder (or to taste), 1 teaspoon grated fresh ginger, 1 tablespoon each of lemon juice and chopped fresh chives. Mix thoroughly and pour dressing over the chicken pieces. Sprinkle with 1/4 cup chopped walnuts. Serve as is or with noodles or rice.   Serves 4

ASIAN CHICKEN SALAD

Remove skin and shred meat of one BBQ chicken. Mix together 1 crushed clove garlic, 2 tablespoons soy sauce, 2 tablespoons white wine vinegar, 1 tablespoon each of fish sauce (nam pla), lemon juice, chopped mint and chopped coriander. Add 2 Lebanese cucumbers, sliced, 1 small red capsicum, sliced, 1 cup bean sprouts and 1 small red onion, finely chopped, to chicken. Pour sauce over and mix well. Serve immediately.   Serves 4

CHICKEN NACHOS

Remove skin and shred meat of half a BBQ chicken. Place 150 g corn chips into a shallow ovenproof dish, allowing them to cover sides. Spoon over 450 g can refried beans. Top with chicken and 1 small green capsicum, thinly sliced. Pour over a 200 ml jar taco sauce and sprinkle with 1 cup grated cheddar cheese. Cook in microwave oven on Medium-high for 5 minutes, until cheese has melted. Serve hot, topped with a spoonful of natural yoghurt or sour cream   Serves 4

CHICKEN JAFFLE

Remove skin and shred meat of half a BBQ chicken. Butter 4 slices of bread on one side, and spread the other side of two of the slices with French mustard. Top with chicken, thinly sliced tomato, 1/4 cup chopped ham or cooked bacon, and sliced cheddar cheese. Season to taste with freshly ground black pepper. Place remaining slice of bread on top, buttered-side up and cook in a jaffle iron or sandwich maker for 3 minutes or until golden brown. Serve immediately.   Makes 2

CHICKEN SALAD

Remove skin and shred meat of one BBQ chicken. Place the shredded chicken into a large mixing bowl and add 1 punnet cherry tomatoes, halved, 1 stick celery, thinly sliced, 1 medium carrot, thinly sliced, 1/2 cup black olives and 1 avocado, sliced (optional). In a small jar mix 3 tablespoons olive oil, 1 tablespoon white wine vinegar, 2 teaspoons freshly chopped mint, salt and pepper to taste, shake well. Pour the dressing over the chicken and combine well. Arrange on a bed of mixed lettuce leaves and serve immediately.   Serves 4

CLUB SANDWICH

Remove skin and shred meat of half a BBQ chicken. Fry 4 rashers of bacon, rind removed, until crisp; drain on paper towels. While the bacon is cooking, mix together 1/4 cup prepared mayonnaise, 1/2 avocado, mashed, and 1 tablespoon wholegrain mustard. Toast 4 slices of rye bread, and thickly spread two of the slices with mayonnaise and avocado mixture. Top with chicken, lettuce, sliced tomato and bacon. Season to taste with salt and freshly ground black pepper. Place remaining slice of bread on top; cut through diagonally.   Makes 1

CREAMY LEMON CHICKEN

Preparation time: 10 minutes
Total cooking time: 8 minutes
Serves 8

2 large barbecued chickens, hot
1 lemon
60 g butter
1/3 cup plain flour
2 cups chicken stock (see
   page 11)
2/3 cup cream

1 tablespoon chopped fresh
   chives
1 tablespoon chopped fresh
   basil
1 tablespoon chopped fresh
   parsley
salt and freshly ground black
   pepper, to taste

➤ CUT EACH chicken into quarters. Keep warm in oven.

1 Remove rind from the lemon with a vegetable peeler. Slice rind into long thin strips.

2 Heat butter in a medium heavy-based pan; add flour. Stir over low heat for 1 minute or until mixture is lightly golden.

3 Combine chicken stock, cream and rind and gradually add to pan, stirring until mixture is smooth. Stir constantly over medium heat 4 minutes or until mixture boils and thickens. Stir in herbs, season to taste. Pour over chicken and serve immediately.

COOK'S FILE

Storage time: Sauce can be made a day ahead. Store, covered, in refrigerator. Reheat gently without boiling.

1

2

3

ORIENTAL CHICKEN AND NOODLE STIR-FRY

Preparation time: 15 minutes
Total cooking time: 10 minutes
Serves 4

1 barbecued chicken
1 medium onion
1 medium carrot
150 g dried flat Chinese
  noodles
1 tablespoon oil
1 clove garlic, crushed
2 teaspoons curry powder
2 teaspoons bottled crushed
  chilli
1 large red capsicum, thinly
  sliced
150 g snow peas, halved
3 spring onions, sliced
2 teaspoons sesame oil
1/4 cup soy sauce
salt, to taste

➤ REMOVE CHICKEN meat from bones; discard bones.

1 Slice chicken into thin strips. Cut onion into thin wedges and carrot into long thin strips.

2 Cook noodles in a medium pan of rapidly boiling water until just tender; drain well.

3 Heat oil in wok or heavy-based pan, swirling gently to coat base and sides. Add onion, carrot, garlic, curry powder and chilli. Stir until aromatic and onion is soft. Add noodles and remaining ingredients. Stir-fry over medium heat 4 minutes or until heated through. Season to taste. Serve immediately.

COOK'S FILE

Storage time: Cook this dish just before serving.

Variation: Any other vegetables can be added to this dish.

1

2

3

CHICKEN PROVENÇALE

Preparation time: 15 minutes
Total cooking time: 15 minutes
Serves 4

1 large barbecued chicken
1 tablespoon olive oil
1 medium onion, chopped
2 cloves garlic, crushed
2 large red capsicum, thinly
    sliced
425 g can tomatoes
1 tablespoon tomato paste
1/4 cup sherry
1/2 teaspoon sugar

1/3 cup shredded fresh basil
    leaves
1/2 cup pitted black olives,
    halved
salt and freshly ground black
    pepper, to taste

➤ PREHEAT OVEN to moderately
slow 160°C.
1 Cut chicken into eight serving
pieces. Keep warm.
2 Heat the oil in a medium heavy-
based pan. Add onion, garlic and
capsicum. Cook over medium heat
until onion is just soft. Add undrained, crushed tomatoes, tomato
paste, sherry and sugar. Bring to boil,
reduce heat and simmer, uncovered,

10 minutes or until sauce thickens.
3 Add chicken pieces, basil and
olives to sauce. Stir until heated
through. Season to taste and serve
immediately with a green salad and
crusty bread rolls.

COOK'S FILE

Storage time: Cook this dish just
before serving.
Hint: Purchased, hot, cooked chickens should always be eaten promptly.
Whole chickens can be reheated in
the microwave. Remove from wrapping, place on a plate and cover with
plastic wrap. Microwave on Medium
for 5–6 minutes or until heated
through.

ORANGE AND APRICOT CHICKEN

Preparation time: 5 minutes
Total cooking time: 10 minutes
Serves 4

1 orange
3/4 cup (120 g) dried apricots
1 cup orange juice
2 teaspoons seeded mustard
1/2 cup chicken stock (see
    page 11)
3 teaspoons cornflour
2 tablespoons water
1/2 cup sour cream
1 tablespoon chopped fresh
    chives

1 large barbecued chicken, hot
salt and freshly ground black
    pepper, to taste

➤ REMOVE THE RIND from the
orange with a vegetable peeler and
slice into long thin strips. Cut apricots into thin slices.
1 Combine dried apricots, juice,
mustard and rind in a medium
heavy-based pan. Stir over medium
heat for 3 minutes or until apricots
are soft. Stir in chicken stock. Blend
the cornflour with water in small
bowl or jug until smooth. Add to pan,
stirring for 2 minutes or until sauce
boils and thickens.
2 Add sour cream and chives and
stir over low heat, without boiling,

until sauce is heated through. Season
to taste.
3 Cut chicken into eight portions.
Place on a serving platter or individual serving plates. Pour sauce over
and serve immediately.

COOK'S FILE

Storage time: Cook this dish just
before serving.
Hint: Always blend cornflour with
cold water, because hot water will
make the gluten in the flour expand
quickly and form lumps. Add cornflour mixtures gradually to hot cooking dishes, stirring constantly until
liquid has thickened.
Variation: Add mango chutney or
sweet chilli sauce to the sauce.

*Chicken Provençale (top) and
Orange and Apricot Chicken.*

1

2

3

4

CHICKEN AND PEPPERONI WITH PASTA

Preparation time: 20 minutes
Total cooking time: 15 minutes
Serves 4

½ barbecued chicken
500 g pasta spirals
50 g pepperoni
1 medium green capsicum
1 tablespoon oil
1 medium onion, sliced
¼ cup white wine
¼ cup chicken stock
2 teaspoons Dijon mustard
2 tablespoons cream

salt and freshly ground black pepper, to taste

➤ REMOVE MEAT from chicken carcass; discard bones. Cut chicken into strips.

1 Cook pasta in large pan of rapidly boiling water with a little oil added until just tender. Drain and keep warm.

2 Slice the pepperoni and cut the slices into thin strips. Cut capsicum into thin strips.

3 Heat oil in a large, heavy-based frying pan and cook pepperoni, onion and capsicum over medium heat for 2 minutes or until the vegetables are just tender.

4 Stir in white wine, chicken stock, mustard and cream, simmer gently for 2 minutes. Do not boil. Add chicken; stir to heat through. Season to taste. Place the pasta in a large mixing bowl. Pour chicken and sauce over and stir to combine. Place on a serving platter or individual serving plates. Serve immediately with hot crusty bread.

COOK'S FILE

Storage time: Cook this dish just before serving.

Variation: Add sliced zucchini, mushrooms or green beans, if liked.

TOMATO CHICKEN CURRY

Preparation time: 10 minutes
Total cooking time: 15 minutes
Serves 4

1 barbecued chicken
2 tablespoons oil
1 onion, sliced
2 cloves garlic, crushed
2 teaspoons grated ginger
2 teaspoons curry powder
410 g can tomatoes, crushed

250 g cauliflower, cut into florets
2 sticks celery, sliced
2 tablespoons ground almonds
salt, to taste

➤ CUT CHICKEN into 10 portions.

1 Heat oil in a large heavy-based pan. Cook onion and garlic over medium heat for 1 minute, or until just soft. Add ginger and curry powder; cook a further 1 minute.

2 Stir in tomatoes, cauliflower and celery. Bring to boil, then reduce heat and simmer, covered, for 5 minutes. Stir in ground almonds.

3 Add chicken pieces to pan, stir to coat with sauce. Simmer, covered, a further 5 minutes or until heated through. Season to taste. Serve with steamed rice.

COOK'S FILE

Storage time: Cook this dish just before serving.

Variations: Fresh chicken pieces can be used in this recipe. Trim off excess fat; cook over medium-high heat for 10 minutes or until cooked through, and continue Step 1.

Add parboiled, peeled and chopped potato or pumpkin in Step 2, if liked.

1

2

3

CHICKEN AND ASPARAGUS GRATIN

Preparation time: 10 minutes
Total cooking time: 30 minutes
Serves 6

1 barbecued chicken
425 g can asparagus spears, drained
485 g can creamy chicken and corn soup
1/2 cup sour cream
2 spring onions, sliced diagonally
1 medium red capsicum, thinly sliced
salt and freshly ground black pepper, to taste
1 cup grated cheddar cheese
1/2 cup grated parmesan cheese
1/2 teaspoon sweet paprika

➤ PREHEAT OVEN to moderate 180°C.

1 Remove meat from the chicken carcass; discard bones. Slice chicken finely.

2 Line the base of a large, shallow ovenproof dish with chicken; top with half the asparagus. Combine soup, sour cream, spring onions, and capsicum; season to taste and pour over chicken.

3 Arrange remaining asparagus on top of the chicken mixture and cover with the combined cheeses. Sprinkle with paprika and bake for 30 minutes, until top is golden and bubbling. Serve immediately.

COOK'S FILE

Storage time: Cook this dish just before serving.
Variation: Cream of mushroom soup can be used instead of chicken and corn, if liked.

1

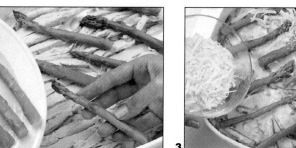

2   3

INDEX

| 1 cm |
| 2 cm |
| 3 cm |
| 4 cm |
| 5 cm |
| 6 cm |
| 7 cm |
| 8 cm |
| 9 cm |
| 10 cm |
| 11 cm |
| 12 cm |
| 13 cm |
| 14 cm |
| 15 cm |
| 16 cm |
| 17 cm |
| 18 cm |
| 19 cm |
| 20 cm |
| 21 cm |
| 22 cm |

USEFUL INFORMATION

All our recipes are thoroughly tested in our test kitchen. Standard metric measuring cups and spoons approved by Standards Australia are used in the development of our recipes. All cup and spoon measurements are level. We have used eggs with an average weight of 60 g in all recipes. Can sizes vary from manufacturer to manufacturer and between countries; use the can size closest to the one suggested in the recipe.

Australian Metric Cup and Spoon Measures

For dry ingredients the standard set of metric measuring cups consists of 1 cup, ½ cup, ⅓ cup and ¼ cup sizes.

For measuring liquids, a transparent, graduated measuring jug is available in either a 250 mL cup or a 1 litre jug.

The basic set of metric spoons, used to measure both dry and liquid ingredients, is made up of 1 tablespoon, 1 teaspoon, ½ teaspoon and ¼ teaspoon.

Note: Australian tablespoon equals 20 mL. British, US and NZ tablespoons equal 15 mL for use in liquid measuring. The teaspoon has a 5 mL capacity and is the same for Australian, British and American markets.

Weights

Metric		Imperial
120 g	=	4 oz
180 g	=	6 oz
240 g	=	8 oz
300 g	=	10 oz
360 g	=	12 oz
420 g	=	14 oz
480 g	=	1 lb
720 g	=	1 lb 8 oz
1 kg	=	2 lb 2 oz
1.4 kg	=	3 lb
1.9 kg	=	4 lb
2.4 kg	=	5 lb

Measures

1 cm	=	½ in
2.5 cm	=	1 in
25 cm	=	10 in
30 cm	=	12 in

Oven Temperatures

Electric	C	F
Very slow	120	250
Slow	150	300
Mod slow	160	325
Moderate	180	350
Mod hot	210	425
Hot	240	475
Very hot	260	525
Gas	**C**	**F**
Very slow	120	250
Slow	150	300
Mod slow	160	325
Moderate	180	350
Mod hot	190	375
Hot	200	400
Very hot	230	450

British and American Cup and Spoon Conversion

Australian	British/American
1 tablespoon	3 teaspoons
2 tablespoons	¼ cup
¼ cup	⅓ cup
⅓ cup	½ cup
½ cup	⅔ cup
⅔ cup	¾ cup
¾ cup	1 cup
1 cup	1¼ cups

Glossary

Australian	British/American	Australian	British/American
Unsalted butter	Unsalted /sweet butter	Eggplant	Aubergine
125 g butter	125 g butter/1 stick of butter	Essence	Essence/extract
Bicarbonate of soda	Bicarbonate of soda/ baking soda	Plain flour	Plain flour/all-purpose
Caster sugar	Castor sugar/superfine sugar	Self-raising flour	Self-raising/self-rising flour
Cornflour	Cornflour/cornstarch	Snow pea	Mange tout
Capsicum	Sweet pepper	Zucchini	Courgettes/squash

Murdoch Books® Food Editor: Kerrie Ray
Family Circle® Food Editor:
    Jo Anne Calabria
Recipe Origination: Tracy Rutherford
    Tracey Port, Jodie Vassallo, Voula
    Mantzouridis, Wendy Berecry
Home Economists: Tracy Rutherford, Voula
    Mantzouridis, Melanie McDermott,
    Rebecca Clancy, Alex Grant-Mitchell
Photography: Joseph Filshie
Cover Photography: Phil Haley

Editor: Rosalie Higson
Design and Finished Art: Marylouise Brammer
Step-by-step Photography: Reg Morrison
Food Stylist: Carolyn Fienberg
Food Stylist's Assistants: Jo Forrest,
    Jodie Vassallo

Publisher: Anne Wilson
Publishing Manager: Mark Newman
Managing Editor: Susan Tomnay
Art Director: Lena Lowe

Production Manager: Catie Ziller
Marketing Manager: Mark Smith
National Sales Manager: Keith Watson

National Library of Australia
    Cataloguing-in-Publication Data: Chicken
    recipes. Includes index.
ISBN 0 86411 358 7
    1. Cookery (Chicken). 641.665
First printed 1994.
Produced by Mandarin Offset, Hong Kong.

Published by Murdoch Books®, a division of Murdoch Magazines Pty Limited, 213 Miller Street, North Sydney, NSW 2060, Australia. © Photography and illustrations: Murdoch Books® 1993. All rights reserved. No part of this publication may be reproduced, stored in any retrieval system or transmitted in any form or by any means, electronic, mechanical, photocopying, recording or otherwise without the prior written permission of the publisher. Murdoch Books® is a registered trademark of Murdoch Magazines Pty Limited. Distributed in UK by Australian Consolidated Press (UK) Ltd, 20 Galowhill Road, Brackmills, Northampton NN4 0EE. Enquiries – 0604 760456.